Challenging
Make
Champions

by Fr. Cedric Pisegna, C.P.

St. Michael's Church New Lothrop, Michigan

How Adversities
Can Elevate You

Challenges make Champions

Live With Passion!

1
WEAKNESS=POWER

There is no doubt we are made for more. From the moment we are born we move and grow and reach. Humans have moved from the independence of caves to the organization of cities, and technology has exploded as we apply ourselves and move forward. We have an innate desire to want to achieve more fully and become more completely. We aren't satisfied unless we accomplish. We have dreams to fulfill and a character to develop. We want deeper, more fulfilling experiences with God.

In short, our life's meaning and purpose is to *become*. Paul wrote about this important truth when he prayed: "May God who began a good work in you bring it to *completion* on the day of Christ Jesus." (Phil. 1:6; italics added) This prayer is echoed again when he writes, "May God sanctify you through and through. May your whole spirit, soul and body be kept blameless at the coming of our Lord Jesus Christ." (1 Th. 5:23)

Life is about changing, growing and moving toward something. Many aren't sure what their purpose is. Others have some type of purpose, but their destination is fruitless. It is important to find authentic meaning and strive toward it. God has revealed to me there are three main areas of life we must focus on and strive to grow in:

- Our relationship with God
- Character development
- Realize your potential: Live with Passion

If you want to live a significant life that will bear fruit in eternity, concentrate on these three areas. Days and months come and go. Seasons change. A variety of experiences and people enter our lives. Through all the kaleidoscope of events and circumstances we must not lose sight of this emphasis. Proverbs tells us "Without a vision the people perish." (Pr. 29:18) Unless you keep this vision before you, you will be adrift and wander aimlessly, like most of humanity. People without a vision will perish, but those with a true vision will prosper.

The Holy Spirit comes to give us correct vision, as well as focus. The great announcement of Pentecost was, "Your young men will see visions and your old would dream dreams." (Acts 2:17) The Spirit of God gives and affir·· s dreams and visions that are authentic and lasting.

> It is God who gives us his vision for our life as well as the power to carry it out.

The Holy Spirit comes to motivate us and empower us to become all we can be and realize our potential. We are not left alone to fumble forward in darkness. Rather, God himself illumines us with the truth of real purpose. In addition, God is at our side assisting us and helping us become. We must cooperate with this supernatural grace in order to fulfill God's will for our life and accomplish our destiny. This life transformation is accomplished with God through our ordinary life experiences. It is God who gives us his vision for our life as well as the power to carry it out.

God wants to transform your life. Jesus was always preaching about personal change and growth in holiness. Most times we think about life transformation happening on the mountaintop, such as Jesus on the Mount of transfiguration. On Mount Tabor in Galilee, his face shone like the sun and his clothes became dazzlingly white. The voice of God was heard and the glory cloud seen in this stunning theophany. While change does occur in the glorious high moments of life, I've discovered that most of life is lived in the valley.

"Even though I walk *through* the valley of darkness, I fear no evil, for you are with me." (Ps. 23:4; italics added) God is always taking us "through" from one place to the next in our lives. In our journey of growth we become acquainted with and learn to trust in God as we face the valleys of life. As we endure and stay steadfast, we develop character and realize our potential through God's blessing. God has promised to be "with" us helping us to the other side. It is the "going through" that is beneficial.

God has not promised to take us around, underneath or above, but through. For a while this "vale of tears" is our temporary home as we journey to the Promised Land. It is in the valley that we learn and grow and become. Mountain moments, few and far between, strengthen us to go through the dark times. It is the dark times of life that can be revolutionary. When you are in the valley there is nowhere to go but up.

This book will help you to see that it is in adversity and affliction that you can be elevated. The elevation that I speak of has to do with our true purpose: depth with God, growth in character, and the realization of your potential.

Valleys are usually places lush and full of growth. We Passionists have a retreat center in Sacramento, California. I will never forget the first time I flew there. I was sitting by the window of the aircraft and I looked down over Lake Tahoe as we headed West. As we descended toward the airport I was struck by how green and lush the landscape was. The Sacramento valley is known for its agriculture. Its golf courses are lovely and contain some of the fastest, purest greens I have ever putted on. It is a beautiful, fruitful area.

God's will for us is to "bear much fruit." President John F. Kennedy said, "Don't pray for an easy life, pray to be a strong person." He knew that true strength is forged in difficulties. You don't know who you are until you grieve, have your patience tested, and suffer physically. You learn about your resolve to be faithful when feelings are withdrawn. Your potential is put to the test when you hit walls.

One of my favorite leisure activities is listening to music. Music lifts me and helps me to relax. I have a number of favorite songs, and one of them is by former Beatle Ringo Starr. The song is, *It Don't Come Easy*. I play that song over and over because I like the melody. But it is the truth of the words of that verse that attracts me. I know that no good in life comes easily. If a deep relationship with God, character development, and realizing your potential were easy, everyone would be doing it. Virtue has value because it is difficult to obtain.

Power in Weakness

Lest you think authentic goals are achieved solely through our own abilities, the Scriptures tell us otherwise. God seems to delight in allowing his power to flow through our emptiness, brokenness, inabilities and afflictions. God can and does work through our abilities, but it is our "weaknesses" that gives God ample room to move. Give God who you are but also give him who you are not.

The stories of how God uses weakness and affliction abound in the Scriptures. Through a stuttering murderer God spoke to an obstinate Pharaoh and set an enslaved nation free. God used a young boy who was rejected by his own family to slay a feared giant. A crucified carpenter from an obscure village redeemed the world.

Paul the apostle recounts his afflictions in many places in his writings. He endured shipwrecks, beatings, snakebites, hunger, as well as long prison stays. While he was in chains, the Word of God was not fettered. It was as if the chains and sufferings became a catalyst to the message b,eing spread more widely. Paul had a mysterious affliction that scholars today still mull over. It could have been an eye ailment. Remember, at his conversion, something like "scales" fell from his blinded eyes. (Acts 9:18) Whatever his ailment, Paul asked for the suffering to be removed. We read, "I was given a thorn in the flesh to torment me. Three times I begged the Lord to take it away." (2 Cor. 12:7-8) God gave him an interesting response, "My grace is sufficient for you. For in weakness, my power reaches perfection." (2 Cor. 12:9) God's grace works powerfully not so much when we are in control, but when we are out of control. Our sufferings are mysteriously an entrée for God to work in us and through us.

> *God's grace works powerfully not so much when we are in control, but when we are out of control.*

Let the Weak say "I am strong." (Jl. 3:10)

My ministry among those in the Twelve-Step program confirms it is in brokenness and so-called "weakness" that God works powerfully. Often significant life changes and even religious conversions come when a person bottoms out or comes to the end of himself. An intervention by family members can be eye-opening. The so-called weakness of hitting rock bottom can lead to the humble admitting of an addiction and actually allows God to work in ways where he was previously blocked. Flaws can lead to favor. Weaknesses can make winners.

Bill Wilson was a man who was born in Vermont in 1895. He struggled with drinking and ended up in the hospital. He had hit rock bottom because of his inability to control his drinking. He was depressed, hopeless and full of doubts. In his desperation he cried out to God to show himself to him. Suddenly he was touched by God's light. In his own words, "I was caught up in an ecstasy and I felt the presence of God." Bill W., as he is known, went on to found Alcoholics Anonymous, which has helped millions of people find sobriety. He said the purpose of A.A. is for people with an addiction to come into recovery. But its main purpose is for people of all walks of life to have an "awakening" with God.

This understanding gives a whole new meaning to the phrase, "A chain is only as strong as its weakest link." Perhaps it is the weak links in our lives that will make us even stronger.

When I was 18 years old I dated a woman during my freshman year in college. We were in love and dated for nine months. When we broke up, I found myself emotionally devastated. I was without God, adrift in my purpose and felt empty and broken inside. I had betrayed the God of my youth by my lifestyle and suffered from an overload of guilt. Little did I know but this inner devastation would be the catalyst for me to turn to God. It was precisely my weakness that catapulted me to a conversion and a whole new relationship with him. God worked through my powerlessness and heard my prayer of desperation.

When I took my SAT's for entrance into college, I did not do well in my English scores. I tested much better in mathematics and knowing that I majored in business studies. While English is my first language, I didn't read all that much and certainly had no interest in writing. Yet, here I am writing my nineteenth book! In addition, I travel around the United States preaching, and my television programs air around the world. Couple that with the panic attacks I suffer because of my fears and insecurities. Who would have thought that those were the ingredients that I needed to be a witness to the world?

Once Paul discovered the secret of how God worked, he began to actually boast of his weaknesses so that the power of God would work through him even more! (2 Cor. 12:9)

While I don't boast of my weaknesses, I'm allowing myself to be more vulnerable before others. I've found that God works in mysterious ways through my humanness. I can't tell you how many people write or email me thanking me for sharing my vulnerabilities. We are all cut of the same cloth. In some ways, the story of one is the story of all. Sharing our flaws is how we relate to each other! We are all in the same boat. While everyone doesn't have the same affliction, we are all human and everybody's got something. Often in my personal appearances people who have read my books or watched me on television see my program and say, "I feel like I know you." My stories document my strengths and mostly my weaknesses. I'm really not afraid of what people think. I'm trying to relate to others. St. Paul of the Cross said our life is like a laboratory. You experiment and tinker around in there and report your findings to others. I don't mind sharing my humanness and even my sins if it will help others. My goal is to reach out and touch people.

One of my greatest challenges as a preacher is creating and preaching new material. It is easy and comfortable to rely on the tested, tried, and true sermons. But even those were new at one time. When I preach something for the first time, great trust in God is needed. I put myself out there and launch into the deep not knowing for sure what is going to happen. I don't have the talk memorized through repetition. My turns of phrases and transitions aren't as smooth as they will eventually be. My talk won't be polished and I am not sure how I will come across.

When I am in that situation, I always feel weak. Sometimes I feel like I bomb. But what is interesting is that I've learned to trust that even though I feel weak when I am preaching, God is working. When the polished facade is stripped away, an honest sincerity and meekness arises. I preach from my heart and gut. I sense God can work more powerfully through my perceived weakness than he will through my polished talks. God honors the risk and the commitment I give, as well as the uncertainty, and touches people.

I remember giving a new talk once as a young priest. I was giving a mission with another priest in Kentucky. As I preached I looked out at the crowd there was absolutely no reaction. I doubted and felt like no one was getting it. I lost confidence and cut the talk short. I have this philosophy, "When in doubt, punt." I bailed. The senior priest I was with at the time looked at me and wondered why my forty-minute talk only lasted twenty minutes. The talk was a lead-in to confessions. I was struck by how powerful the confessions were. One woman told me the only reason she came to confession was because of my talk. Later on, I shook my head in amazement at how

God worked in that situation. In my perceived weakness and powerlessness, God moved.

So, I know that, no matter how I feel, power is made perfect in weakness. I still trust my feelings when I preach. My instincts have made me better and better as a speaker over the years. However, when push comes to shove, preaching is a supernatural event wherein I must lose control. Above all, I rely upon God to make something good happen in the hearts of people. I'm always creating new homilies so it is exciting to see what kind of effect my words will have on people. Whenever I feel weak, I trust something good is happening.

Even after all these years as a priest I still don't feel all that comfortable preaching. I'm always nervous to some degree. While I may do very well I actually feel very needy and insecure. I'm an introvert and to go before people and give like I do is very draining for me. When I finish preaching I am usually hungry and depleted. It is very hard for me to shake hands afterward and wonder how my talk affected each person. I smile and do my best, but sometimes I wonder why God didn't call someone else. I think the reason God uses me isn't because, like some, I enjoy hearing myself speak. Rather, for me I am launching into the deep and risking failure and rejection. God sees the sacrifice and works through my humanness.

One of the reasons I am shy and introverted is because when I was young I developed acne. I didn't have the worst case of it as a teenager, but bad enough. I can't tell you how emotionally crippling a disease like this is. Having blotches on your face cuts to the core of your self/body image. While I have nice facial features, my complexion years later is not good. We all struggle with lines and sagging skin, but many of my pores have been damaged and now lines are developing where they shouldn't be. I have dark circles under my eyes and at times the last thing I want to do is go public!

While we all want to show our best face, I've noticed that this weakness makes me more approachable. Other people who have similar conditions aren't intimidated by me. Although I'm on television, I'm not "untouchable" like some. While I want to look like a model (and do from a distance) up close it is a different story. People always tell me I look tired, but I think they do a double take. Perhaps they think, "He is just like me and look what he is doing!" I trust that even in this powerlessness, God works powerfully. If God can work through my flaws, he will work through yours. You really can turn your scars into stars.

> In powerlessness, God works powerfully.

Television preacher Joyce Meyer says something interesting. "Give God who you are as well as *what you're not.*" It took me a long time to understand that saying. I'm used to offering God my gifts so he can use them. I'm now learning to offer God my flaws so he can use them too! In the Old Testament God only wanted the sacrifices of animals that were perfect and without blemish. Now, in Jesus, God accepts blemished sacrifices. Not only does God accept them, he works through such sacrifices. We are invited to offer ourselves to God as a living sacrifice even if our sacrifice has blemishes. God has a way of turning our blemishes into blessings.

The Weaker Sex?

Speaking of Joyce Meyer, I'm amazed at how God is using women in our day and age. Joyce is one of the premier proclaimers of the Gospel on television. We are used to hearing that women are the "weaker" sex. Perhaps they can't perform physically in sports like some men, but they have proven over and over again they are in no way weaker. The women's suffrage movement had to overcome many barriers. Finally, women were allowed to vote and they continue to strive for equal rights and equal pay. Women today have come a "long way baby." As I am writing this, the national election was just held and for the first time Congress is now composed of over one hundred women! This was unheard of years ago. Can it be long before we have our first woman president?

In church circles, women bring a unique perspective and keen insights. They offer practicalities in daily living sometimes not brought out by their male counterparts. For too long we were only given the masculine perspective. Now we are getting a fuller picture. I studied at the Catholic Theological Union at Chicago. I was taught how to preside at Mass. Our teacher, a Catholic sister, is an esteemed liturgist and brought many insights to presiding, by being an observer for all those years. Also, one of my homiletics professors was another Catholic sister. Her approach to the craft of preaching mixed her professionalism with a captivating femininity.

I was also taught the Bible by women, as well as men, dedicated to the truth of the Scriptures. The women in particular showed their love of the Bible through the obvious hardships they had to endure to get to where they are today. I'm glad those in charge of my formation allowed us to be exposed to various unique ways of thought that wouldn't have been considered years ago.

I've heard from a number of women who sense a call from God to preach and proclaim the Gospel. Janice

Carleton is the wife of my producer and one of my ministry partners. They live in Portland, Oregon, and are the parents of four grown children and grandparents of six. Janice feels a strong call from God to lead retreats and inspire people. I'm so encouraged that she gives retreats in the Portland area and across the country, even when it isn't popular to have a woman lead these days of recollection. Her book, *God Speaks to Ordinary People - Like You and Me* includes many stories about family and how God works in the ordinary. I'm proud of her and her accomplishments for the kingdom of God.[1] Thank God for the many women today who are finally coming into their own! God certainly knows how to work through the "weaker" sex. Time and time again he says, "You go, Girl!"

I heard it said that God formed Eve from Adam's rib, not to walk before him or behind him, but to walk *alongside* of him. Thank God for the many women today who are finally coming into their own!

To be human is to experience weakness. We experience trials, difficulties and sufferings. There are divorces, deaths of family and friends, as well as physical afflictions. There are societal injustices, addictions, accidents and economic inequalities. We struggle with insecurities and inadequacies. Yet, despite all this, and *because of* all these things we can achieve and see God work through it. Divorce, death, addictions, and physical maladies can help us to reorient our lives and can lead to self-discovery. So-called handicaps can catapult one to a successful life. You've probably heard of the Napoleon complex or syndrome. This is when a person compensates for a handicap in life by overcoming it. History says Napoleon became a great military leader

1 www.janicecarleton.com

because he was short in stature. It was precisely his perceived disability that thrust him into greatness.

It is when we embrace and don't deny the adversities of our life that we can overcome them and accomplish much. In other words, our challenges can make us champions.

Evidence of this truth about weakness abounds in the Bible. Paul wrote, "Jesus was crucified in weakness but raised in power. Although we are weak, we will have power." (2 Cor. 13:4) God, on purpose, chose the foolish things of the world to shame the wise. God chose the weak to shame the strong." (1 Cor. 1:27)

The Great Reversal

Jesus' most eloquent sermon was his Sermon on the Mount in Matthew. Luke's version changes some of the words and has a plain as its setting. In his teachings Jesus exalts what the world considers of little value and contradicts worldly wisdom. Jesus proclaims the poor in spirit as blessed. He tells us the meek will inherit the earth. He pronounces "Woes" to those who are rich, full, laughing and spoken well of. (Mt. 5, Lk. 6) When we approach Christianity, we need common sense, but sometimes the common sense we learned from the world simply doesn't work.

Jesus' words fly in the face of what our culture tells us we need to succeed and be happy. Christianity brings a wisdom that is not of this world. Instead of "might makes right" and "only the strong survive" we are taught, the last will be first.

Paul spoke of this wisdom when he wrote: "Jews demand signs and Greeks seek wisdom, but we preach

Christ crucified, a stumbling block to Jews and folly to Gentiles, but to those who are called, both Jews and Greeks, Christ the power of God and the wisdom of God. For the foolishness of God is wiser than people, and the weakness of God is stronger than people." (1 Cor. 1:22-25)

Just as God redeems the world through a man broken on a cross, he works in and through our brokenness also. When it comes to the Bible, we have to see with new eyes and think new thoughts. Jesus told Peter this when Peter tried to get Jesus to avoid the cross. Jesus then said, "You are not thinking as God thinks, but the way people do." (Mt. 16:23) The world is full of "flawed" thinking.

When I was a seminarian, our liturgy teacher gave us an intriguing article by the Jesuit Michael J. Buckley. The article was entitled, *Because Beset By Weakness,* and had the paradoxical subtitle: Are you *weak* enough to be a priest? I am well aware of the ethos of our culture. Perhaps it is expressed in this song by Sheryl Crow: *Are you strong enough to be my man?*

We like success, sleek looks, and people who are comfortable in their own skin. We are attracted by these attributes. But weakness? Insecurity? Ambiguity? Uncertainty?

Actually, Buckley's article reinforced notions I had believed for years. We don't have to have it all together to be chosen and used by God. In fact, as I've stated above, God, *on purpose*, chooses the weak and lowly.

The article uses as its foundation the truth from Scripture that Jesus can deal gently with humans because he himself is beset with weakness. (Heb. 5:2) This "weakness" doesn't mean Jesus sinned, but rather he was subject to temptation, experienced fear, anguish, betrayal, anxiety, loneliness, and desolation. He was sensitive, familiar with hurts and pain, and was vulnerable in his human state. Jesus knows what it is to be human and can relate to us on our level. As Scripture says, "We have a high priest who can *sympathize*." (Heb. 4:15; italics added)

The author of the article made the assertion that the priesthood of Jesus Christ flows from humanness and vulnerability. The vocation to priesthood is familiar with suffering and has it as part of its essential structure. I remember I once saw a head-turning billboard by the side of the road. It was an advertisement for vocations to the priesthood. It showed a bloodied Jesus hanging on the cross in torment. Underneath were the haunting words, "Be a priest like me."

Any human being experiences ambiguity, mystery and uncertainty. None of us knows ourselves completely. We all have a future that is uncertain. Life is full of unanswered questions, and everyone experiences fear, anxiety, stress, confusion and interior struggles. Some religious people deny this side of themselves because it makes them feel uncomfortable. They feel they should have all the answers and allowing themselves to be human mitigates the certainty of faith. But I have found that true faith develops when you are honest with yourself and real. Our fragmentation is our authentic starting place.

When they sin some excuse themselves by saying, "I'm only human." Sinning isn't what makes us human, in fact sin is dehumanizing. When we say we are fully human we are simply admitting we are limited and don't have all the answers. Authentic humanity recognizes our limitations and genuine needs.

Exploring what it means to be human calls to mind a person's view of Christology (the study of who Jesus was.) A "high" Christology tells us Jesus was aware of his mission from God and had all of the answers as soon as he was able to reason. The emphasis is on his divine nature and communion with God. A "low" Christology means Jesus was fully human and had to grow, learn and experience life like we do in order to come to fuller understanding. The emphasis is on his human nature. Of course Jesus was a mysterious mix of the two and so are we. For too many years theologians stressed Jesus' divine nature. Now the pendulum has swung in the other direction. Accentuating Jesus' humanity not only makes sense, but helps us to relate to him at a deeper level.

I've seen many ministers who love to pontificate from high platforms. They like being above people, and some talk down to others. There are those who hide behind the collar and feel secure in their titles and rank. (This was behind Jesus' statement: "Call no man on earth 'father.'") They minister out of black and white certainty and wouldn't dare share their inner struggles. They are afraid of being human lest there be a perceived flaw or weakness that might water down their witness. They have to come across as always having all the answers and having it all together. They fool some, including themselves, but not God. This is some of what Jesus was driving at when he called the religious leaders hypocrites and talked about their desire to be noticed with long, flowing garments and tassels. (Mt. 23:5)

My training and formation as a priest never denied my human side. In fact we were urged to explore our humanity and talk things out. We were asked to go to counseling so we could come to grips with our fears, insecurities, and uncertainties. We were expected to embrace our feelings, any inadequacies and self-image struggles and come to fuller wholeness. Far from denying our humanity, it is healthy to face it. This is how we come to psychological health. Yet, we are also divine. We spend a lot of time in formation getting in touch with the mystical. We pray, read, and talk things out with a spiritual director. Like Jesus, we are a mysterious mix of faith and fear, certainty, and unknowns.

While some only minister from the platform of strength and certainty, I believe we must be "weak enough" to be a priest. Weakness is a bridge to compassion. Priests should be on the same wavelength as the people, able to understand what others are going through. Relating to others is one of the key "geniuses" to preaching. Priests should preach with the authority of their office and the truth of the Gospel. But, we ought not preach using words and stories people can't relate to. We should preach from our own experiences and be fully human. We need to be relevant, and our pertinence lies precisely in our humanity. When a person denies their own humanity, they lose touch with the people they minister to. One way I try to illustrate this truth is when I distribute communion. Communion, of course, is the body of Jesus, broken and given for all. Some communion ministers like to stand on steps or ledges and be on a higher level looking down. I always make sure I step all the way down (even if the pastor next to me stays up on the step) to be on the same level with the people.

Along with my humanity, the Spirit of God has divinized me. I am both human and divine. The Eastern Fathers talked about this process of divinization as "godding." In saving us, God has made us partakers of his divine nature. We have God's nature within us that can bring us deep revelation and understanding. Because of this divine insight, we can become convinced of our rightness in a way that comes across as arrogant.

Unfortunately while some minister out of this "certainty" at the expense of their humanity, others are all too human and they leave no room for the absolutes. We need a proper blend of both. The Spirit of God brings faith, certainty, clarity, wisdom, assurance, and revelations. I minister out of this side of myself of first importance. You can't give what you don't have, but when you have it, by all means, give it!

I proclaim the truth of the Gospel with the authority and boldness that can only come from the Holy Spirit. I share revelations I have received such as my near-death experiences, heavenly dreams, and my experiences with the Holy Spirit himself. It is divinization, not sin, that makes us fully human. As a priest, I minister out of a platform of certainty and authority that inspires and intrigues many. This authority from God gifts me to preach with gravity, intensity and passion. I give what I have been given: salvation, rebirth, and a personal relationship with God. But, I also minister from the level ground of being totally human with sufferings and experiences that people can relate to. Ministers and priests today need both. God works through our strengths as well as through our weaknesses.

Come to the Mystic

Our afflictions and weaknesses have great value in our spiritual advancement also. Besides leading to an initial conversion, they can help us with ongoing conversion. As I stated before, I sought God after I broke up with my girlfriend during my freshman year in college. I was devastated and lonely inside. I was surrounded by people at college but had few friends. I had no real goals and was adrift. I had forsaken the God of my youth. Ironically, my need for forgiveness as well as my emptiness and isolation were precise ingredients that led me to God. I came empty and needy, but God filled me.

God hears the cry of the poor. He listens to teenagers who are floundering but want to understand. I experienced a life-changing rebirth. God touched me through my brokenness and continues to work through my fragmented self. Since the days of my initial conversion it is my emotional and physical sufferings that propel me to new levels with God.

Afflictions of various sorts can have the function of waking us up and moving us toward God. God working in our weakness is a spiritual law attested to in the Bible. "Before I was afflicted I went astray, but now I obey your word." (Ps. 119:67) God doesn't necessarily give us these afflictions, they come to everyone by being human. But, God in his graciousness understands and uses adversities to draw us to himself. All you need to do is talk to someone in the Twelve-Step program and they will attest to this truth.

In a similar way, once we are on the right path, (after our initial conversion) God uses our humanness and weaknesses in our "ongoing" conversion. The great journey of our life is from self*ish*ness to self*less*ness. We are moving from love of things to love for God and this journey takes a lifetime. Perhaps our greatest idol is our "self." Our culture teaches us to be self-made men and women and to be confident in ourselves. We are taught to rely on our self.

As I notice people, I see many put their confidence in their looks or physical fitness. Those with higher education can easily put their stock in their degrees and intelligence. Others find their security in their family, marriage as well as friendships. There are some who find self worth and value through their athleticism or other talents such as music, art, or writing. Still others find their confidence in their pedigree or net worth. In addition we put confidence in the flesh when we begin to rely on our judgments, ideas and opinions excessively. We can become prideful and overly self-reliant. In our fallen humanity our reasoning can be flawed. Our looks, abilities, intelligence, and net worth are all unstable and fading. Only God is rock-solid and sure. It is fine to be confident, but it should be a God confidence that leads to an inner poise that will endure and not crumble.

Only God is rock-solid and sure.

Paul listed his esteemed religious credentials. Piously, he had it all. He had the proper upbringing, prestigious schooling, and high religious standing. Unfortunately his pedigree led him to a prideful, narrow-minded way of thinking that ended with him murdering the deacon Stephen. Mercifully, Jesus touched Paul and changed him. He grew to the point where instead of having confidence in his credentials (flesh) he wrote, "Whatever gain I had, I counted as loss for the sake of Christ." (Phil. 3:7) When touched by Jesus, he placed no confidence in his religious standing and pedigree (flesh), but in Jesus.

Afflictions burst the bubble of our exaggerated self. Paul learned this truth by his experiences of suffering. He wrote:

The afflictions we suffered in Asia made us so utterly, unbearably crushed that we despaired of life itself. We felt that we had received the sentence of death itself; but that was to make us rely *not on ourselves but on God* who raises the dead. (2 Cor. 1:8-9; italics added)

The Scriptures advise, "Put no trust in princes in whom there is no mortal help." (Ps. 146:3) Even the rich and the royal are bound to collapse and fail.

Whenever I experience emotional and physical turmoil it has the effect of making me quiet. As I reflect deep within, I find myself relying less on my own self and surrendering more to God. I know my physical sufferings are the birth pangs of the dying process. Relying on self is like trusting in shifting sand. "All flesh is grass" (1 Pet. 1:24) "We are but a mist." (Ja. 4:14) We are doomed to perish. I have become acutely aware of the brevity of my life measured against the span of eternity. Psalm 90 proclaims it is wisdom to realize our finitude: "Teach us to number our days that we may gain wisdom of heart." (Ps. 90:12) Rather, the more I suffer the more I distrust my own self and rely upon God who "raises the dead." God, not ourselves, is our only hope. Suffering puts me in touch with my mortality. The first time I saw a grey hair on my head I laughed and thought, "O No, I'm going to die." For some, when they suffer they blame God. Either they think, "How can God do this to me?" Or, "Any God that would allow me to suffer isn't a God I want to know." Sufferings are neutral emotionally. It is how we choose to think about our afflictions that matters.

The Return

God works through our weaknesses and afflictions to draw us to himself. The classic case is the story of the Prodigal Son. His hunger and poverty caused an awakening and brought him back to his father. When sufferings move us toward God, the union deepens as we progressively turn to him over and over again in personal surrender. We are experiencing our own passion as we advance in our dying process. A mystical oneness can occur as we put no confidence in our flesh but transfer our allegiance completely to God. The martyrs were a witness precisely because they trusted more in God than they did themselves. Our weaknesses can turn to strength. God's grace *is* sufficient. The journey of our life is to bring us to wholeness in God. One of my favorite verses is this: "I trusted in God even when I said in my alarm, I am sorely afflicted." (Ps. 116:10) Our weaknesses can bring a depth with God we would have never known without them.

This book is all about identifying how God works through afflictions, sufferings, and so-called weaknesses. Not only does God work through our sufferings, he makes us triumph in them! What are your weaknesses and afflictions? Is it something physical, a relationship problem, something spiritual? Something else? Get in touch with your weaknesses and major afflictions. I want you to know God will use these to draw you to himself. He will work through them to lift you higher and make you a champion. The world says are you *strong* enough? Christianity teaches are you *weak* enough?

2
CHALLENGES MAKE CHAMPIONS

In the first chapter I wrote about how our weaknesses can be a catalyst for God's activity. Another way to describe weakness is *challenge*. We all have challenges in life whether they are physical or professional. There are hurdles we must navigate in life, and hurdles can make us heroes. Many discoveries are made in difficult times. For example, I've read that as our water supply lessens, water purification plants and creative desalination strategies are being developed. Necessity is the mother of invention, and we can choose to become champions in our challenges. Problems can promote us. In fact, we don't necessarily accomplish things in spite of our obstacles, but precisely *because* of them. Obstacles are actually opportunities for advancement.

I have discussed the importance of focus. At the time of this writing, I watched a program on the Discovery channel about Nik Wallenda and his high-wire walk between two high-rise buildings in Chicago. Nik is one of the members of the famous flying Wallenda family who have performed many death-defying stunts.

This particular stunt was filmed on live TV. He did one walk on a tightrope between two buildings over 600 feet high. Scores below watched as he walked the tightrope on a chilly, windy November night in Chicago. People gasped and murmured as he performed this walk. He ended up being successful and safe. I watched on live TV and thought, "If something happens, will they turn the cameras away?" There was no need to. Then within minutes, Wallenda did an even more difficult walk at a similar height, this time, blindfolded! Even though his visual field was blocked, I noticed he placed a speaker that emitted an intermittent beeping sound at his destination. Although he couldn't see, he could hear, and he concentrated on the continuous beep. There was a hush in the crowd. His own people looked worried as he stepped out onto the wire, blindfolded. This death-defying walk was successful, too. He was able to face his fears, overcome them, stay steady, and accomplish the feat. He attributed his success to his faith in Jesus, his preparation, as well as his *focus*.

Our focus in life is crucial in determining our success.

Our focus in life is crucial in determining our success. We must focus on our destination and not the distractions that abound. In this book we are focusing on the three main qualities that will make our lives successful. The world has its definition of success, and usually it has to do with acquiring wealth, having friends, power, and fame, as well as being happy. As stated before, I've discovered the ingredients to true success depend upon:

- Our relationship with God
- Character development
- Realize your potential: Live with Passion

I want to explore the second and third areas in this chapter. Of course, all three areas overlap to some degree.

Do you have passion in your life? What gets you up in the morning? What is your source of motivation? I believe if you have purpose, passion will flow. Some people's passion is to make a lot of money. Many strive for power or fame. Others want to get married and raise children. Some want to advance as far as they can in their field. Many have music, art, writing or acting as their passion.

As Christians, our prime purpose should be to please God. When you are passionate for God you strive to get to know him. In addition, you serve others, avoid sin and grow in virtue. In a nutshell, in order to please God, you develop as a person. You are anointed to become Christ-like. Jesus was virtuous, wise and realized his potential, and we are to emulate him. A wonderful energy flows from this purpose. If you don't have purpose, you lack drive and energy. If you know anything about my ministry, I have adopted this saying as its foundation: Who you are is God's gift to you; who you *become* is your gift to God.

Passion!

The name of my television program is *Live with Passion!* I chose this because I noticed that as life went on and routines developed, many lost their enthusiasm and initial zest for life. They became satisfied with what they achieved early on in life and never pressed on for more. For example, in a marriage, once the honeymoon stage was over, things slowed down. In the business world, after one got a job he settled in and was not ambitious and willing to do what it takes for a promotion.

When I talk about living with passion, I mean we must be enthusiastic about life. I love it when I meet people who are excited about life! The word enthusiasm means "in God." God provides energy and passion to advance your life and help you be your best, but you must agree with God and invest in yourself. On the day of my ordination, as I lay prostrate before God's altar, I promised God I would live with passion. I spent many years studying and being formed for the priesthood. I didn't want to just attain priesthood and stop there. I saw priesthood as the launching pad, not a landing pad. In my mind I've never arrived at priesthood—I am becoming a priest every day. True priesthood entails work, continual growth, and on-going formation. If God has called you to marriage, be enthusiastic about it! Your wedding day was the beginning, not the end.

We all have routines and limitations. Don't let them determine you, but push the boundaries and live a full life. If you are single, divorced, or widowed, be interested in your education, your talents, and your gifts. Invest in yourself. Put yourself at the service of God and others and believe in yourself because you are a temple of the Most High God.

On the home page of my website, www.frcedric.org, I have an inspirational saying or word appear each time you visit. When you log on you might see: "achieve!" The next time: "make something!" Or, "take risks"; "apply yourself"; "be ambitious;" "be creative"; and so on. My goal is to try to inspire people to live passionately, not passively. It is so easy to settle for the status quo, but God wants us to move as far forward as we can.

As I live my own life I've discovered that God has an individualized plan for me, and my own choices determine whether or not that plan will come to fruition. I am motivated to realize as much of my potential as possible. I've seen God give me more and more power, influence, contentment, and happiness as I have given my heart to his will. The secrets of happiness and self-fulfillment lie in cooperating with God's will. Every saint stressed that God's will was their delight. Jesus said God's will was his "food." (Jn. 4:34) In other words, doing God's will nourished him.

God has a plan and destiny for you. The purpose and meaning of your life is to find his individualized will for you and walk in it. We pray this every day, in the well-known 'Our Father', "Father, *your will be done.*" Achieving our destiny

> God has a plan and destiny for you.

is a major part of God's plan for us. God wants us to take the talents he placed within us and give back to him in return.

The parable of the talents in Matthew is a story we've all heard. (Mt. 25:14-30) Many struggle to understand this story, but I think it is one of Jesus' best. God is seen as an investor who at least wants interest out of our lives. When he sows in us he expects a return. That's why this saying rings true, "Who you are is God's gift to you, who you become is your gift to God."

A talent is a huge amount of money. Some scholars say it is up to twenty years' worth of wages! The bottom line: God has placed expensive gifts and abilities in each of us, and it is up to us to develop these gifts or they will remain unused and undiscovered. Even your ability to see, hear, and move is part of God's gift to you. Many come to the end of life filled with regrets, wishing they had done more and realized their talents while they had time. Make use of your talents and gifts from God so that you arrive at the end of life fulfilled.

We see what we are—our external body and the moods and emotions we experience each day. But God sees what we *could* be. When he looks at us, God sees our potential and knows what he has put in us. The story of David being chosen from amongst his older brothers teaches us that God looks not just at the externals, but at our hearts. (1 Sam. 16:7) For example, we just see the ground, but God sees the oil underneath. We just see dirt, but God is aware of the diamonds being formed in darkness. We see harrowed ground but God sees the seeds sprouting. We observe rushing streams, but God knows the treasures of gold nuggets lying within. We see our human body, and God sees our potential.

Taking Chances

A key ingredient in developing your potential is taking a risk. A young woman came to me wondering if she had a call to religious life. I shared, "You probably won't see God's will written in black and white. Look within and pay attention to your desires. God works through our inner yearnings. Take a risk. Step out. Take a chance. Otherwise you will never know." The call to religious life is actually a call to greatness. God is inviting us to stretch and go beyond the ordinary to realize who we can be. Similarly, with marriage, spouses are being invited to give themselves to each other and to the community in selflessness. Any call demands risk. People get cold feet because they are taking a big chance. But risk is precisely what life asks of every one of us, no matter the call.

In the Lord's parable, the man who buried his talent did so out of fear. Fear is the great destroyer of destiny. People are afraid of failing, afraid of what others think of them, and afraid of trying new things. Unless you face your fears and be willing to fail, you will never advance. Did you know the fact that you can walk means you are resilient? Everyone of us fell when we learned how to walk. Our repeated failures meant repeated attempts, and our failures eventually led to the ability to walk. You can fail forward.

In addition, we are told the servant was lazy. Our feelings will always try to drag us down. It is easy to sit on the couch and watch television. If you allow your feelings to rule your life you will never amount to anything. Rather, get in touch with your innermost desires. Who do you really want to be? Let your heart drive you, not your feelings. You must be ambitious, take the initiative, be determined, apply yourself and be industrious.

Passion is the opposite of passivity. It is the Holy Spirit who leads us in these virtues, but we must cooperate with the movements of grace within. In the parable, we see that God applauds industry and rewards initiative and risk with double blessings.

Recently, I was asked by a friend of mine to join the Knights of Columbus. I meet men who are Knights in each parish where I preach. They are the salt of the earth. If you are not familiar with them, the Knights are a Catholic fraternal benefits organization composed of men from every walk of life. These men are pro-life and proclaim the Gospel through helping others. I'm always impressed by their sacrificial dedication. For many years I balked at joining any organization, but when it came to the Knights of Columbus, I signed up. I became a Knight not only because I want to participate in the plentitude of good works they offer, but because I want to support Knights everywhere I go, and tell them, "I am one with you." Also, I want them to know I applaud their passion.

The bottom line: God is pleased when we risk, invest and live with passion. We've all heard the saying, "Nothing ventured, nothing gained." When you live a fearful, lazy, mediocre life, you thwart the blessings of God. You aren't happy because you know you aren't developing your talents and realizing your potential. When you work and take the initiative, you come to a new self-understanding and come into your destiny.

The parable of the talents has two possible endings. The sad ending is the weeping and gnashing of teeth because of the pain of regret. It is bitter to realize you had a chance and didn't take it, and devastating to see what you didn't become. The other ending is to hear those gracious words, "Well done, good and faithful servant. Come into the joy of your master!" These famous words are the number-one thing people say they want heard when they come before God in judgment. Which will you hear, fearful or faithful? You were created for greatness. You are made in God's image and he has put vast treasures of talent in you. Now is the time to be bold, take the initiative and live with passion!

> *Now is the time to be bold, take the initiative and live with passion!*

Our motivation in life should be to please God, realize our potential, and influence the lives of others. We live with passion, not out of guilt, but to push the boundaries and reach for the stars. You don't know who you really are until you push yourself. Diamonds are mined deep below the earth's surface and the only way to find them is to dig. Similarly, you are a diamond in the rough. Your talents are just waiting to be mined.

Many at this moment are nearing the end of their lives in nursing homes and hospitals. Their bodies are wearing out and they are losing strength. Perhaps even worse than the physical sufferings they have to endure is living with regret. Toward the end of life people always review their pasts and think how they could have been different. Many regret they didn't risk, or try, or push the boundaries of their lives. They tell others, "If I had it to do again I would…"

I want to live my life with no regrets. When I am old and unable to do what I now do, I want to know I took the initiative and created opportunities. What will put a smile on my face then is the knowledge that I risked, worked, achieved, and influenced the lives of many. I did what I could with what God gave me. This is what Paul was driving at when at the end of his life he recited his monumental achievements and said, "I fought the fight, I finished the race and kept the faith." (2 Tim. 4:7) There is deep satisfaction in those words.

A life of passion means work, creativity, applying yourself, and digging deep. Determination, drive, ambition, and gaining momentum are very important. Many people shy away from work because they just want an easy life. I like Caleb, who, we are told, had a "different spirit." When he came toward the end of his life he said, "Give me a mountain!" (Jos. 14:12) It is tempting to avoid the inclines of life, but when we work out on a treadmill, we find it is the incline that builds muscles and greater endurance.

I want to make something very clear. While I try to motivate people to be the best they can be and achieve, I am not a motivational speaker per se. I am a Catholic priest. The foundation of any accomplishment and influence is not self but *God*. I don't preach self-actualization as much as God actualization. I love this verse: "We are more than conquerors *through him* who loves us." (Ro. 8:37; italics added) The word in the Greek for conqueror or victor is one with which we are familiar. It is "nike." Most people know that the sports equipment giant, Nike, uses that same word. They market, "buy our product and you will be victorious." But the word in the Greek is *hyper* nike. Think of children with ADD, who are so full of energy and difficult to settle down. In God we have supernatural energy to be passionate.

The word also means that we not only have the victory, but we win *exceedingly* or *overwhelmingly*. If we were a football team we wouldn't only win, but win 70-0. God doesn't just want us to squeak by in life; ours should be a clear and decisive triumph. In other words, Jesus didn't die for us to have a mediocre life, but one that is successful spiritually, attitudinally, and professionally. We *can* defeat the many forces that come against us and be the person God calls us to be. Often, God will even use negative and dark forces to transform us and catapult us to greater things. This is what happened with Jesus. "Jesus disarmed the powers of evil, triumphing over them by his cross." (Col. 2:15) The method of his so-called demise was the instrument of his victory.

My ministry comes with a lot of stress and pressure. I have a highly visible platform and I speak face to face to tens of thousands of people every year. I write books, air on television and radio, as well as social media. While no one likes pressure or stress, I've actually found these platforms push me to do even better. It is under pressure that some of my best episodes and talks emerge.

> *Irritations are actually invitations to a better life.*

While no one likes the discomfort that pressure brings, we all enjoy the fruit of being pushed. Irritations are actually invitations to a better life. We all know that diamonds are created under the connection of time and compression. Pressure can lead to your best result.

I communicate through books, television, and radio because I discerned a call from God to reach out to people. I have taken the initiative and worked hard to reach beyond the walls of the church to influence the lives of others. Because of this outreach, I draw a large response from people. I have many letters and emails to respond to. Often I think, "Why do I keep taking this initiative? It only means more effort and work. In some ways I am digging my own grave..." Is being passionate worth it?

Here is what I've determined. *Boredom is overrated.* If doing a lot of work is a burden, mediocrity and regret are the greater pain. I'd rather endure the stress of pressure and burden of work than the pain of regret and an uninteresting life. We all have to endure our pain in life. No matter how you live life there will be pain and disappointment of one kind or another. I want my pain to count for something. I'd rather brave pressure, stress, and work than live a bland, mediocre life. My sufferings touch people, glorify God, and lead to the realization of my destiny and happiness, and I bear fruit now and in eternity. I have decided to choose life and live, and not look back. Work doesn't hurt you, it helps you. We are made for more and will never be happy without achievement and striving for success. There is the pain of work or the pain of regret. Which will you choose?

Attitude

In order to realize our potential and live the destiny God has for us, we must avoid excuses. Common excuses are: "I don't know what my talents are. I'm too busy. I'm suffering and overwhelmed. I'm not as gifted as others. I can't do it. How do I know if it is really God's will?" I've discovered negativity is one of the greatest enemies to passion and self-fulfillment. A positive attitude not only leads to great joy, it works! Being positive will help you develop your potential and turn a tough situation inside out. The altitude adjustor on an airplane can bring an aircraft higher or lower in flight. Similarly, our beliefs, moods and determination can have an effect on our spiritual altitude. Airplanes can take off from rough runways such as grass, dirt, snow or even water, and so can we.

I grew up in a little town south of Springfield, Massachusetts, named Feeding Hills. Feeding Hills is a suburb of a larger suburb, Agawam. When I went to grammar school, I noticed a statue in the town square. The statue was of Anne Sullivan, Helen Keller's teacher. She taught Helen how to communicate. This was extremely difficult because Helen became blind and deaf at a very early age. How do you teach someone who is blind and deaf to communicate? Anne had a major breakthrough usir water. Once Helen associated the texture of water with the word Anne spelled into her palm, she progressed rapidly from there.

As Helen Keller grew up, she not only learned to communicate, but actually allowed her disabilities to motivate her to reach out to others. She ended up publishing twelve books and several other articles. Her writings were all positive and motivational. In *Three Days to See* she challenged us to appreciate our vision and other senses. Here is an excerpt:

I who am blind can give one hint to those who see: Use your eyes as if tomorrow you would be stricken blind. And the same method can be applied to the other senses. Hear the music of voices, the song of a bird, the mighty strains of an orchestra, as if you would be stricken deaf tomorrow. Touch each object as if tomorrow your tactile sense would fail. Smell the perfume of flowers, taste with relish each morsel, as if tomorrow you could never smell and taste again. Make the most of every sense; glory in the beauty which the world in all the facets of pleasure reveals to you through the several means of contact which Nature provides.

Helen is urging us to look and listen with new eyes and new ears. What we take for granted can come alive if we appreciate it and give thanks to God, who gave us these gifts. Helen had an adventurous spirit that accomplished much, even though she was disabled. Actually, disabled people talk about being "*other-abled*." She didn't allow disability to bring her down, but to lift her—and us—up.

> *What we take for granted can come alive if we appreciate it...*

Like Helen Keller, my dad had a problem with his eyes. He grew up with healthy eyes and he joined the U.S. Navy as a young man and became a Seabee, fighting in the South Pacific theatre. One day he was on the deck of one of the ships and the crew was working on some molten metal. He happened to be nearby when a piece of the metal flew out and landed in his left eye. Unfortunately, it seared his pupil shut. The best surgeons used laser to try to open it, without success. He was only able to see the faintest of light.

Dad was honorably discharged from the Navy and he got married. He now had a wife and family to support. He had a gift for carpentry and invested himself in his talent, all with one eye. He didn't allow his disability to stop him. Not only was he a builder, he was a master craftsman. I've seen him craft tabernacles, lecterns and wooden altars for churches. He also built houses (including our own) and room additions. I know, because I used to work with him as a young man. By the way, that's how I knew I had a call to the priesthood. I was a lousy carpenter! Dad had that wonderful gift, but my interests lay more in sports. I am not very mechanical nor good with my hands.

In all the many years I worked with my father, I never once heard him complain about his eye. Because of his blindness, he lost the muscular tension in his left eye and his eye wandered. I noticed and asked him what happened. He told me the story of his being wounded. I'm proud of him because of the great job he did with one eye. Most aren't great carpenters with two eyes, but he did it with one. Not only that, he never complained. He accepted his disability and made the most of it.

I've often imagined what it would be like to be blind in one eye. Besides losing one-half of your field of vision, you lose a major portion of the 3-D depth perception that is so needed in carpentry. Dad overcame this disability and even used it to make him better. It is said when you become blind, your senses of hearing and imagination sharpen. He developed keen visual instinct and woodworking savvy. Dad taught me an unforgettable lesson about keeping an optimistic attitude and making the most out of your life.

Problems and adversity can have an impact on your relationship with God. I've already discussed how the apostle Paul wrote that his crushing afflictions served to make him rely upon God who raises the dead. In addition to deeper trust, sufferings can unite us to God mystically.

St. Paul of the Cross waxes eloquently about sufferings in just about all of his spiritual direction writings. In one of his many letters he wrote,

> I wish that all men could understand the great favor that God grants them when, in His goodness, He sends them suffering, and especially suffering

devoid of all consolation; for then the soul, like gold which is purified in the fiery crucible, is cleansed, made beautiful, detached from earthly things, and united to the Sovereign Good, without even being conscious of it.

Paul of the Cross also wrote about the concept of mystical death. One of his favorite expressions was "to die with Christ." In one letter to Sister Maria Cherubina Bresciani he wrote,

May the mercy of God grant you still more time in life so that you can become completely crucified with the Divine Spouse by means of mystical death, death to everything that is not God, with a continual detachment from all created things, wholly concealed in the divine bosom of the celestial Father in true inner solitude. Do not live any longer in yourself, but let Jesus Christ live in you in such a way that the virtue of this Divine Savior may be resplendent in all your actions, in order that all may see in you a true portrait of the Crucified and sense the sweetest fragrance of the holy virtues of the Lord, in interior and exterior modesty, in patience, in gentleness, suffering, charity, humility, and in all others that follow.

Our sufferings and trials can actually catapult us to greater heights in God. As we journey through life, we must die to self in order to discover our true self. The spirituality of Paul of the Cross is not one for the faint of heart. It is a call to maturity and the radical growth that comes through suffering. The writing and wisdom of many saints such as St. John of the Cross with his "dark night of the soul" have embraced the truth that suffering can lead to a higher life.

St. Paul of the Cross was a great spiritual director. He had many intense mystical experiences of God, especially in his younger days. But as he grew older, these consolations and comforts were gradually withdrawn. Many pray only when good feelings accompany the prayer. Some pray only when they seem to be getting answers from above. Not Paul. What made Paul saintly as well as a compassionate spiritual director was his faithfulness and endurance in prayer, even when the consolation wasn't felt. He didn't always see the answers to his petitions, but he remained faithful.

He lived to be 81 years old, and some historians say for the last 30-40 years of his life he embraced the mystical death and dark night of the soul and felt very little. Paul didn't see the withdrawal of comfort as a punishment, but as a grace to enter into. Besides being able to relate to others who were experiencing such spiritual difficulties, Paul allowed the dry desert to purify him. He discovered a deep union with the crucified Christ in his own sufferings. His spiritual challenges made Paul a champion. In difficulties, where others give up, he looked up.

> *Feelings are fickle, but faith is forever.*

One of my favorite sayings is: "Feelings are fickle, but faith is forever!" This rings true especially in the spiritual life. Feelings are wonderful, but it is faith that endures.

Growing up in Massachusetts, we had some very cold and snowy winters. My dad generously bought our family a snowmobile. I used to love to race around on the snow. The interesting thing was, the colder it got, the better it ran. Snowmobiles run on air-cooled engines and their performance actually suffers when it is warm outside. I can remember some days and nights when the temperatures were frigid, below zero. That snowmobile would sing and zip faster than ever. I would just touch the throttle and it would hum. Oddly, when it was above freezing, the same machine would be sluggish and sound like it was bogged down. In the mechanized world, some machines are designed to work better in adverse conditions.

Notice, it was the freezing frigid temperatures that made the snowmobile go further, faster. Airplanes are designed to take off faster into the wind. Similarly, adversity in life can lead to efficiency and elevation. While we can find our Shepherd in pleasant places, it is as we go through the valley of darkness and disappointment that we really get to know him.

Benefits of Darkness

Sometimes the darkness in life is good. When we are conceived, we are molded and fashioned in secret, in the darkness of our mother's womb. Seeds that are planted germinate and sprout in the darkness. We sleep better and pray more easily when our eyes are closed. The deterioration of culture in Europe in the so-called dark ages gave rise to the advancement of the Renaissance. As the old saying says, it is usually darkest right before the dawn.

I'm fascinated by how professional photographers develop their film. After spending hours shooting just the right photos, they take their treasured film into a dark room. It is in the dark, in a place devoid of light, where they wash this valuable film in a special solution. Given time and care, the photos begin to develop. Any light at the wrong moment will actually spoil the project. Through the process, shadows and light become apparent and more and more pronounced. Similarly, our character becomes more pronounced and develops in the darkest moments of life. In time, we see who we really are as we are tested by the trials and adversities we face. God knows the exact amounts of darkness and light that are needed at the proper times.

God can work even through darkness, but it is best to focus on the light in your life. I studied theology in Chicago at the Catholic Theological Union for four years. C.T.U. is located on the south side of Chicago, near the science museum and the prestigious University of Chicago. One of my Passionist classmates was from the Philippines. One winter, he began to complain of feeling tired, listless, moody and depressed. He visited a doctor and was diagnosed with S.A.D. (seasonal affective disorder.) One half a million people in the US get this every year and seventy-five percent of them are women. The doctor said, "You are used to the warmth and sunshine of the Philippines. The winters in Chicago are cold, grey and snowy. Your moods are being altered because of all the gloomy days."

The doctor gave my friend an interesting prescription. For a remedy he said, "I want you to take a bright lamp in your room. Turn it on, tilt it up and leave it on all day long, even throughout the night." Do you know this photo/light therapy worked! As he focused on the light, my friend became less moody, had more energy, and became his old self again.

I write this in January and it is cold in Houston. I notice the stray cats love to lay in the sunshine to warm up. Animals are naturally attracted to the light. Light provides photosynthesis for vegetation, and without light, there wouldn't be oxygen for us to breath. I have a plant in our residence where I live. For a while I had it on a shelf away from the window. One day I decided to move it to the windowsill. In a few days I noticed the fingers of the vines started moving toward the window. The plant itself was naturally gravitating toward the light. If we were to watch it on time-lapse video, we would see the plant moving and grasping for the light.

We all have light and dark situations in our lives. Whatever we focus on will determine our mood and how we handle things. While God can work in the darkness, we shouldn't focus on the gloom or get stuck there. If you focus on the dark, like my friend, you will become sad and listless. Jesus said, "I am the light of the world. No follower of mine will wander in the dark. They will have the light of life." (Jn. 8:12)

It is so easy to get stuck in the negative situations in your life. You may be going through physical suffering or relationship and financial difficulties. Perhaps you don't seem to be advancing in your spiritual life. If you focus solely on the externals, like my friend, you will become sad and discouraged. I've learned to focus on what God can do in the hard times, how God can make all things work to good. There is always darkness, but I try to look for the silver lining in every cloud.

I thank God for my athletic abilities. I've always been attracted to sports and participated in just about every sport there is while growing up. As I grew older, I couldn't engage in team sports and narrowed my activities down to golf and running. Everywhere I went I would take my running shoes with me. Whenever I'd preach a mission, no matter where, I'd make sure I ran. Running helped me with stress, got my heart rate up, and enabled me to keep my weight at a good level.

One day I was running down a steep incline in California. The downgrade was over a mile long and I was running at a pretty good clip. When I finished the run I noticed I had pain running down the back of my right knee. In time the pain was chronic. When examined by a doctor I found out I had a tear in my meniscus, the cartilage in the knee that protects the bones and alleviates pain. I ended up having two arthroscopies and the tear developed into full blown arthritis of the right knee.

Five years after those surgeries I was giving a mission in New Jersey and working out in a fitness center there. After my workout, I experienced severe, sharp pain unlike ever before. I was barely able to finish the mission. When I got home I went immediately to my doctor, who suggested I see another surgeon. Our knees each have three compartments and I found out one of my compartments was totally devoid of cartilage and I needed to have a replacement. This partial knee replacement was one of the most traumatic things I have ever been through from start to finish. I found out what I already knew: I don't like being a patient in a hospital.

The surgery was pretty successful, but it took a long time to heal. While there is still some stiffness and pain over a year later, I can function normally and even work out pretty vigorously. One thing I cannot do, however, is run. I was told that I should avoid high impact exercises.

> *Focus instead on what you can do.*

I have come to accept this change in my life, but at first, if I was driving a car and passed a jogger it would devastate me. Over and over again I would think, "Why can't I run? Why did this happen to me? I've always been so healthy." I was grieving growing older and losing the abilities of my youth. One day I was having my usual pity party and

I heard within, "Instead of focusing on what you can't do, why don't you focus instead on what you *can do*?"

I never forgot that voice. That breath of wisdom has helped me to accept my condition and move on. The truth is, I can still do almost everything. I just can't jog or play basketball, softball or tennis. But, I can do everything I need to do, including preach and carry heavy boxes of books for my missions. On top of this, as I said, I can work out pretty vigorously at the fitness center. Whenever I start to succumb to self pity, I tell myself, "Don't go there again. We've been all through this. Focus on the multitude of things you *can* do." Realizing I can still do almost everything has really helped me accept the changes in my body.

Not only that, but my adversity has served to *advance* me. I was actually horrified when my weight ballooned to over 190 pounds after the surgery. I'm used to being in the 170's and have never had to watch my weight. I love to eat, so I was faced with a decision. Was I going to stay overweight and feel unhealthy or do something about it? I am six feet, two inches tall, and while I didn't look that heavy, I know my body, and there were places jiggling and protruding that never used to.

I made the decision not only to rehab my knee, but to work out aggressively. About five times a week I stretch and exercise on the treadmill, bike elliptical, running elliptical and stair master. I use weights to tone my muscles and finish off by swimming many laps in the pool. I push myself and now it has become a lifestyle I have actually come to enjoy. When I don't work out, I miss it! Because of this aggressive lifestyle, as well as being vigilant about my diet, I have whittled my weight down from the 190's laboriously through the 180's to the upper 170's again! It took an entire year and it was hard work, but I feel so much better about myself, and I don't think I've ever been so healthy.

Since golf was one of the major culprits in the demise of my knee, I have made the decision to retire from golf. I love golf, but I'm tired of having back pain, knee pain, hip pain, and shoulder pain. I am finally listening to my body. I may play once in a blue moon, but it is not a part of my lifestyle anymore. I've found now I have so much more time to minister, write, read, and exercise.

My surgery and weight gain actually catapulted me to a healthier level. I choose to focus on the positive and now I avoid excessive eating and sports activities that are harmful to me. I have learned firsthand that at varying ages we can't do what we once did in our youth. My injuries served as a wake up call to let go of some of my less-productive activities and embrace an even healthier lifestyle. At some point in our journey, we all need to face the reality that confronts us as we are growing older. By accepting this, I have let my hurts help me.

At my health club I saw someone wearing a shirt that said, "Champions are made in the off season." You don't see the arduous workouts and training of the Olympians. You only see the results when they compete. But without the preparation there will be no hope for a medal. Football players go through training camp; baseball players have spring training before their season. These times of training are difficult and filled with work. Similarly, my working out and becoming fit has enabled me to be more energetic, passionate and confident of my abilities when I preach. I don't tire as easily and instead feel fit when I stand up and teach. Paul wrote, "Every athlete who competes in the games goes into strict training. They work out to get a crown that will not last; we train to get a *crown that will last forever.*" (1 Cor. 9:25)

Everybody's Got Something

One thing that has helped me is I don't have to look far to know there are always people much more challenged than I. Some are doing incredible things in spite of their disability. A program on ABC that is very popular is *Dancing with the Stars.* Celebrities from the sports or entertainment world are invited to dance with a professional partner in a competition against other stars. The dancers are judged on their abilities by three professional judges as they perform live on national television. This show is highly intensive, competitive and viewed by millions.

In the 2013 season, Amy Purdy was invited to participate on the show. Amy is an athletic young woman who at age nineteen contracted Neisseria meningitis. She was given less than a two-percent chance to live. Because of the effects of this disease, she had to have both legs amputated below the knees. She also lost both kidneys, as well as her spleen. Although the disease ravaged her body, she beat the odds and lived. She challenged herself to move on with her life and strove for goals that able-bodied people struggle to attain. She won medals in three events at the national snowboarding championship, and she is an actress and motivational speaker. When asked to appear on *Dancing with the Stars* and compete against able-bodied people, she deliberated because she wasn't sure she wanted everyone to know about her physical disabilities. Finally, she agreed.

Purdy was paired with dance professional Derek Hough. He had won the winner's trophy with other celebrities five previous times and had retired. He came out of retirement to dance with the program's first double amputee, Amy. She set many records on the show and made it all the way to the finals against two others. In the final program she performed three dances. The three judges gave her perfect tens on two of the dances and 29 out of 30 in the other dance, totaling 89 out of 90. Because of that one point, she finished in second place to another couple who scored a perfect 90. In the minds of many she was the champion, not because of points, but because she had the courage to participate and push her so-called limits.

In one of her final dances, Amy was elevated through the use of a twisting cloth that took her higher as she clung to it. To me, that was symbolic of her whole time on the program. Her disability literally catapulted her to new heights. She inspired millions by her courage, and is now a highly sought-after motivational speaker. Her new book *On My Own Two Feet: From Losing my Legs to Learning the Dance of Life* was recently published.

There was a guest judge on week three of the series: Robin Roberts. of the popular *Good Morning America* program also on ABC television. She recently wrote a book that I read called *Everybody's Got Something*. In the book, she shares how a few years ago she developed breast cancer. She took some time off and was treated with chemotherapy and radiation. The end result was that she overcame the cancer, but a few years later she found out she had bone marrow problems. Your bone marrow is crucial because it produces the needed red blood cells and assists the immune system. Robin needed a bone marrow transplant. Even if you can find a matching donor, the transplant is a risky procedure and dangerous to both parties. Robin's sister Sally Ann turned out to be an exact match and graciously agreed to donate her marrow to her sister.

Robin had the transplant, but it took time to heal. She documents in her book the hardships she went through and how close to death she actually came. It was a dark and hazardous time in her life, to say the least, but she came through it. If you tune in your television in the morning, you will see Robin and her winning smile on your television screen. She continues to welcome people to a new day on a national level. Her dark days of sickness taught her a lot about appreciating the great life she had and now has again. Her faith in God grew ever stronger as she relied on Him to bring her through the darkness. She also learned about the importance of focusing on the positive.

It is in the "going through" where we learn our life lessons and develop our relationship with God. Having a personal relationship with God happens through revelation, in prayer, but especially in our everyday walk.

What attracted me to Robin's book was the title, which she said she got from her mother: *Everybody's Got Something.* I've found this rings true. No matter who you are, where you were born, or how much money you have, you have something that complicates your life. I talk to and pray for people who have heart problems, *Everybody's got something.* cancer, and end-of-life issues. Other struggles include children leaving the faith, divorce, and feeling desolation in prayer. Others are grieving, lonely, depressed, or trapped in an addiction. In the human condition, everybody's got something, and most have more than one thing! There were many inspirational truths revealed in Robin's book that relate to this book. She wrote, "Being optimistic is like a muscle that gets stronger with use. You have to change the way you think in order to change the way you feel."

When I was preaching in Ho-Ho-Kus, New Jersey, I noticed a woman present at each session who was in a wheelchair and had no legs. She was one of the secretaries who worked at the rectory. After one of the services I asked, "What happened?" She said her mother had some type of sickness when she was pregnant with her that led to her being born without legs. I said, "You seem to have a great attitude about it all." She replied, "My mother always said to me, 'Never say you can't do it.'"

I've heard it said there are two people in the world who are absolutely 100 percent right: those who say they *can* and those who say they *can't.*

I received a book in the mail a few months back. It was from a woman who watches my television program, *Live with Passion!* She said she is the wife of a Methodist minister and my program inspired her to rekindle her dreams. She had always thought of writing a book but never did. She finally got to work and stayed determined and wrote, *God Recycles Broken Dreams.* I was so happy to get this book, and I was proud the woman wrote it. I was especially touched when she told me she was 88 years old!

I love the prophecy of Pentecost: *Your young will see visions and your old will dream dreams.* Because of the Holy Spirit you are never too young to have a vision and never too old to dream a dream! Don't think all this positive talk is just for youth. It is for you. Growing older itself can be the challenge that thrusts you forward.

Joni Eareckson Tada is a person who inspires me. I first heard her give her testimony at a Billy Graham crusade before thousands, in person and on television. What inspired me was that she gave her talk in a wheelchair. She grew up as a healthy young woman who loved horses and swimming. In 1967 she dove into the Chesapeake Bay and misjudged the shallowness of the water. She ended up breaking her back and becoming a quadriplegic, paralyzed from the shoulders down.

During the next couple of years Joni (pronounced Johnny) experienced deep sadness, doubt and anger. Finally, she made the decision to make the most out of her life. She had the ability to draw and paint. Now she paints portraits and scenes not with her hands or feet, but with her teeth. These drawings are professional and better than many people can do with their hands and arms. Joni is an author, singer, radio host, and has appeared in movies and been nominated for an Oscar. She is also an advocate for the disabled community. She is a gifted woman, whose disabilities actually elevated her to new heights.

One of the most influential books I ever read was *Man's Search For Meaning* by Victor Frankl. Victor was a Jewish psychologist who was captured and held in a Nazi concentration camp during World War II. In the horrid and depraved conditions of the camp he saw people at their worst and best. He saw some become very selfish and others who were amazingly selfless. The extreme conditions revealed what lay deep in each person. We've all heard stories of people like St. Maximillian Kolbe, who gave his life in the place of another in the starvation bunker. The flip side of Saint Maximillian were people who selfishly hoarded bread and stole from others and even committed suicide as they lost hope.

Along with all the human stories and experiences Dr. Frankl reveals in his book, there are many truths he explained. Perhaps the greatest lesson he learned was about our personal choices. "The greatest of all freedoms is the power to choose our own attitude in any given set of circumstances." This saying has stuck with me for my entire life. It is up to us to search for and discover the meaning of any event we encounter. Once we have meaning, then we can choose our attitude toward the event. It is not the situation itself that determines our response. We choose and determine our response. Circumstances have no power. We have the power to choose.

> *The greatest of all freedoms is the power to choose our own attitude.*

Sufferings Produce Character

A common belief is that being successful or famous brings a person happiness and contentment, yet we know from the experiences of others that success can spoil you and fame can ruin you. Similarly, failure and obscurity can lift you up. It all has to do with who you are at your core, your maturity level, and how you choose to handle things. Paul the apostle learned a valuable secret in his travels and travails. Some expeditions led him to places where he abounded and had plenty. Other travels led him to danger and long prison stays. In the midst of plenty and lack, abundance and want, he learned the secret of contentment. He found deep meaning and significance through his faith in God. He wrote this famous statement: "I can do all things through Christ who strengthens me." (Phil. 4:13) He wasn't talking about accomplishments, which most people interpret in this verse. Rather, he was referring to contentment and attitude in the midst of having nothing or having plenty. Paul displayed this transcendent attitude when he sang in prison and stayed humble despite abundant heavenly visions. Trouble and hard situations can stretch us and bring out the best in us. In fact, the only way we can know who we are deep within is to face travails of every sort. James speaks of this when he writes:

> Count it all joy when you meet various trials, for you know that the testing of your faith produces endurance. And let endurance have its full effect, that you may be perfect and complete, lacking in nothing. (Jas. 1:2-4)

Similarly, Paul wrote: "Suffering produces endurance and endurance produces character." (Ro. 5:3-4)

Endurance is another word for virtue. The writers are saying that tribulations can produce various virtues in us and lead to our becoming better. One of the major areas we must focus on is our character, because character development is crucial if we want to do God's will. In the midst of suffering, being positive, patient, and enduring will forge character within us. Jesus said that it is by patient endurance we will win our souls. (Lk 21:19) Remember, God is a potter who wants to mold and shape us into the image of his Son. He uses our everyday real-life experiences and sufferings to fashion us. Jesus has a heart that is faithful, endures, and is very patient. He handled hardships, trouble and adversity worthily, and it is our goal to be like him.

I wrote this chapter as I was visiting my mother's house. She died a few months ago, and I was staying at the house my dad built and where I grew up. I had one last time to reflect and savor the memories. I stood in my bedroom by my window on the spot where I have prayed countless prayers. It was on this very spot that I prayed about my television dream years ago. I remember asking God to remove this dream if it wasn't from him. Ten years later, as I stood on the same spot and prayed, I couldn't help but review some of the many sufferings and trials I've been through now that broadcasting on television has become a daily reality. These sufferings have produced endurance as well as character in me.

As I stood in my bedroom reminiscing in prayer, I said to myself, "Even though I've been through a lot, I've grown, faced and coped with every challenge and am reaching out to multitudes. Knowing what I know now, if I had it to do again, *I'd still do it."* That was a huge insight for me. There have been so many challenges, sufferings, and difficulties. I wanted to give up numerous times. Even though organizing missions, writing, and television is not easy, with God's grace, I've become indomitable. My dream has become the place where I have become the priest God intended me to be.

If I had it to do again, I'd still do it.

I used to be so negative about myself and suffered from self-image problems in high school. As a freshman, I had a panic attack as I read publicly in front of my high school English class. This traumatic experience devastated me emotionally. I still feel the effects of that failure even today. In college, I was touched by the Holy Spirit and came to discern God calling me to the priesthood. I still had lingering fears and feelings of inadequacy, but I decided to live courageously, step out, and trust God. Although I was afraid, I tried new things, met new people and lived way beyond my comfort zone. Day after day, God was at work in me.

When I was finally ordained a priest in 1991, I stepped up to the plate and did what I feared most: preach. Not only did I preach homilies, I pushed myself to achieve the status of being an itinerant missionary. This is when your full-time ministry is preaching! I knew I had a supernatural gift and people responded positively. I loved the people and wanted to help them long after I visited their parishes, so I began to write books in 1999. Ironically, I never did all that well in my English classes, so writing was a great risk to me. I was afraid that I would start the project and never be able to finish, and I feared people would judge me and see me as unintelligent. But my books turned out to be great projects and they sold like hotcakes at my missions. I continue to write and have watched my progression of thought develop through the years. I've discovered a lot about myself as I write, and I have developed discipline and have a good work ethic. I've expanded my teachings one hundred-fold. I've also discerned the fact, as others have told me, that I am an artist as well as being a priest. I don't draw with pencils or a brush on canvas. I paint with words.

As much as I loved reaching out through preaching and writing to the faithful who came to my missions all across the U.S. and Canada, I kept feeling the tug that God was calling me to do more. I meet so many people on golf courses who used to be Catholic but who no longer attend church. I meet young people who are good people, but have no religion. As I searched my heart, I knew God wanted me to reach out beyond the walls of the sanctuary to people who aren't going to church and who need salvation. After all, we can't expect them to come to us, we have to go to them.

But in order to reach beyond the walls, I had to face a huge wall of my own. I was a Catholic priest with a professed vow of poverty trying to get into a medium that demands lots of money. Television is very expensive. Not only that, I had no outlets to air the programs. In fact, I didn't even have any programs produced! Talk about a wall!

Rather than run, I began to face the walls and the multitude of challenges that getting on television from scratch brought. My missionary zeal and work ethic served me well. I produced many programs despite great hardship and lack of funds, taking the initiative to contact many Catholic stations. I still remember calling them and telling them I wanted to get on their stations. They said, "Who are you?" I was undeterred and zealous. Finally, I produced a pilot series and sent them the programs, whether they requested them or not. Much to my delight, they began airing my programs. A momentum developed and I haven't looked back.

I was able to do many things, but there were doors only God could open. St. Francis is quoted as saying, "Do what is possible and God will do the impossible." God has given me favor, despite all odds. I aired on Catholic channels and some secular stations for six years. I produced, worked, endured, and kept expecting. Then a major breakthrough came.

God opened the door for me to air on the national Church Channel and then the Trinity Broadcasting Network (TBN) itself. As of this writing, I air Sundays at 8 am ET/ 5 am PT. I am one of only two Catholic priests on the largest Christian network in the world, and I represent Catholicism to this largely Protestant audience. More than that, I proclaim the Gospel to many who don't know Jesus. TBN's reach is vast. My program, *Live with Passion!* airs in many nations. I receive emails from as far away as Africa, the middle east, South America and Australia. Talk about going outside the walls of the church! My ministry reaches into homes, hospitals, hotels and prisons with the Gospel of Jesus Christ. I have suffered greatly, but have stepped up to the plate with my dream of changing the world. Archbishop Fulton Sheen rightly said, "This is the age of television." Dreams do come true!

My living in a religious community has been a tremendous challenge, also. I am a religious priest and part of my call is to live with and pray with others. I share everything in common in a professed vow of poverty. As you know, living with people pushes you to become tolerant and forgiving. I live with many personality types from a variety of cultures. Each person has their own distinct way of approaching life and dealing with its challenges. I have been stretched as a person and become generous in ways I never thought I could.

The ministry I've developed and the community life I've vowed myself to is all a result of the challenge of discipleship. *Jesus summons each one of us to follow him.* He makes no apologies for the difficulty of the call. We are following the Son of God, after all. He is worthy of our every effort and energy. Discipleship demands dying to self and living for God and for others. We must

> *Jesus summons each one of us to follow him.*

make a radical surrender of our personhood and time. The challenge of discipleship is life-long and results in closeness to God and eternal life.

Because of the adversities I've faced, I am a different person now and what I've gained from the tribulations of becoming a Passionist priest and TV missionary can never be taken away. My self-image has changed and I know I'll never be the same. My resume has equipped me to face the trials of the future. Challenges have made me a champion.

The challenge of following Jesus is demanding. Through discipleship, I am being changed, and my adversities have truly advanced me. Slowly but surely, through the many events and people in my life, God is shaping me into the image of his Son. This essential truth that God is forming us through our experiences (Ro. 8:28) must be one of the focuses of our life. Paul prayed this prayer filled with insight, "May God who began a good work in you *bring it to completion* on the day of Christ Jesus." (Phil. 1:6; italics added)

> God is forming us through our experiences.

The Power of Positivity

Years ago I was about to speak at a mission. I had my lavaliere mike and replaced the batteries. I always have to make sure to align the polarities on the batteries or the microphone won't work. I must put positive to positive and negative to negative. As I was putting the batteries in the compartment, I heard a still small voice within. "Cedric, you are just like these batteries. You have a positive side and a negative side. Whichever you choose you will become." I have never forgotten that moment. It was absolutely eye-opening and life-changing for me. I have both polarities (extremes) within me, and whichever attitude I choose is totally up to me.

I've determined I am going to be positive! Negativity does nothing but bring me down. I want to realize my potential and destiny and the way to become fully mature is by being positive. We all have the ability to choose optimism and hope. Be careful about how you think - it will become your attitude. Your attitude will determine your character, and your character, your destiny.

It is so easy to focus on the negatives in life. We live in an imperfect world, and even the best people have character flaws. Nothing ever happens fast enough, and our dreams seem stuck in molasses as we get older and our health declines The world we live in is full of troubles and problems. It seems like our default setting can be faultfinding, cynicism, murmuring, and complaining. While the people who surround us may be this way, we have to rise above this and choose life. When you follow Jesus there is a better way to live. I call it "kingdom living." Kingdom living means being positive, and having peace, as well as the ability to enjoy your life. (Ro. 14:17)

I came from a good family. My mom and dad always respected me and treated me well. I was given whatever I needed to achieve and advance in life; I was raised in a good neighborhood and had great educational opportunities as I grew. Why, then, was I so negative?

No matter your familial background or place of origin, you cannot be insulated from our culture. Our society is replete with negative trappings. People who surround you make negative comments and think in pessimistic ways. Negativity comes through osmosis. In the world of politics there are smear campaigns; news programs aggrandize violence and sensationalize current events in order to attract ratings. In school, you must choose your friends well, because there are many who aren't motivated and won't accomplish much with their lives. In the workplace envy and backbiting abound. In religious communities, there are those who live glum, downcast lives. Complaining is contagious. Like a cold or the flu, it is easy to become infected with pessimism and negativity.

I used to love to watch Norman Lear's *All in the Family*. If you remember, the show featured Archie and Edith Bunker, as well as their daughter, Gloria, and her husband Michael. Archie was perhaps the most prideful, bigoted, negative man ever represented. He was king of his castle and he never had an unexpressed thought. When I was young, I allowed his way to infect me. I even used to talk like him on occasion.

Because he used his tongue in such a profane way, one episode was particularly humorous. Gloria and Mike had prepared animal tongue for Archie, but they knew he wouldn't eat it if he knew what it was. They therefore tried to distract him as they put the plate down in front of him. He finally looked quizzically at the plate and said, "What is this?" Gloria replied, "Daddy, it's tongue! Eat it, you will like it." Archie retorted, "Tongue? I ain't eating nothing that comes out of no animal's mouth! Edith, go get me an egg!"

Watching programs like this, as well as rubbing elbows with pessimistic people, influenced me. I became adept at seeing the dark lining in every cloud. I even won a contest about complaining! When I was growing up, the Springfield, Massachusetts, newspaper had a daily contest called "Write a Gripe." Each day they would choose a winner and put it in their column. I submitted my gripe, and wouldn't you know, I won! Not only did I get my name in the paper, they even paid me a small amount. My gripe was, "I hate dentists with bad breath!" They showed an artist's rendering of me in a dentist's chair. Hovering over me was a dentist with a visible cloud of halitosis coming out of his mouth. My name and address was clearly shown under the drawing. I was happy to win, but the only problem was, I had to go to my dentist the next week for an examination!

Instead of focusing on the excellent care I was receiving from the dentist, I was thinking more of his imperfections. Instead of giving thanks for having dental care in a world where most don't, I complained. Many complain when it comes to their job, marriage or school. Complaining can be insidious as well as destructive. Paul wrote, "Many of you are not keeping busy, but acting like busy bodies." (2 Th. 3:11) The next time you are tempted to complain, try to realize how many people would love to have your job. Be aware there are many who are single and lonely who pray to have a companion. Appreciate the good life you have.

The Hebrews had seen many miracles from God's gracious hand. They had been forged as a people, redeemed from Pharaoh and liberated through the Red Sea. God fed them with manna and quenched their thirst with water from a rock, and he led them with a cloud by day and by fire at night. Yet, despite all the manifestations of God's goodness, they still murmured and complained throughout the journey. This sin cost many their lives.

I've discovered that no matter what level you have attained in your life it is easy to focus on the negative. I always thought I would be happy if I ever got on television. I discovered that being on TV wasn't the secret to happiness. Rather, it brought more problems, difficulties, and work into my life. It is easy to be overwhelmed by it all and want to give up. Yes, I do have an inner joy from having achieved this level of success, but it is no magic formula to contentment. As I said before, it isn't the level of success or the circumstances that bring true happiness.

The truth is, success has spoiled many. Some have the charisma but not the character to handle prosperity. When it comes to achievement, higher levels will bring new devils and will call you to be even more responsible when it comes to gratitude and relying on God.

The Power of Thanksgiving

It is the will of God for us to give thanks in (not for) all circumstances. (1 Th. 5:18) There are problems and difficulties at whatever level you have achieved in life. The way to find contentment is to focus on God and to give thanks for the good things no matter your difficulties. This is the mark of a true champion. The missionaries Paul and Silas, when chained in the darkness of a prison cell, sang at the midnight hour and the Lord freed them from bondage. God knows how to break open any locked door and make you a witness as you express gratitude. Sometimes you just have to stir yourself up to give thanks, even if you don't feel like it. You have to rise above your feelings.

It is the will of God for us to give thanks.

My Mom died just before I began writing this book. She was ninety years old and died from complications resulting from aortic valve heart surgery. God gave me time to help me grieve and relive some pleasant memories. I had lived there with my mom and dad for some thirty years on and off. I had so many gracious memories of growing up in their home. That house was my home and a place I loved to come back to in order to rest and celebrate the holidays.

I stood in my mother's empty bedroom and memories of her flooded my mind. In many ways being in the house, and especially her bedroom, was my connection to her presence. As I stood there I thought, "How can I leave this house? It is my connection to Mom and Dad and so many past memories." Then I heard within, "Instead of focusing on the past, concentrate on your future." I thought, "I don't want to, the past was so good." I immediately thought, "The future will be even better!" This is hope. We don't need to remain mired in the past, but believe the future holds good things for us.

As I stood by Mom's bed I thought, "How can I move forward from the past?" Immediately came the answer, "Through thanksgiving." Instead of lamenting the losses I celebrated the graces. Thanksgiving is healing. God works through gratitude to help you move past the losses of life.

Many of you have lost parents and the homes where you grew up, and have felt the pain of what I am describing. God is faithful to bring us through to a better day as we give thanks. Only memories remain, but the future is bright. God has given us a gracious past, but an even more glorious future remains. To be human is to have to make peace with the past and move forward in life. God is always doing something new and gives us new seasons in which to grow and encounter even more blessings.

Every year at Thanksgiving I wonder about atheists and agnostics. They have no one to give thanks to. Our national holiday is empty for people who don't believe in God. They gather and sit with relatives and while Thanksgiving brings them together as friends and family, it is so hollow without its true meaning: giving thanks to God Almighty. Our Thanksgiving roots can be traced to the Pilgrims in Plymouth, Massachusetts, who in 1621, feasted and gave thanks to God for a blessed harvest.

(In a little known earlier Thanksgiving, Spanish Catholics landed in St. Augustine in 1565 and feasted with the Timucuan Indians.) Since 1863 Thanksgiving has been an annual tradition in the US due to presidential proclamation, and has been celebrated on the fourth Thursday in November since 1941.

In the Catholic Church the font and summit of the expression of our faith is Eucharist, or the Mass. Eucharist comes from a Greek word that means thanksgiving. Mass is a prayer. We pray to the Father through the Son in the Holy Spirit. There are many songs and prayers that comprise the Mass. The crescendo is the Eucharistic prayer itself. Through the act of giving thanks, something miraculous happens; ordinary gifts of bread and wine are transformed into the very body and blood of Jesus Christ. We follow the pattern of the Master who gave thanks at the Last Supper. Earlier in his ministry, when holding a few loaves of bread and some fish, Jesus gave thanks and they multiplied to feed thousands. The act of giving thanks ruptures the ordinary and ushers in the supernatural.

> *The act of giving thanks ruptures the ordinary and ushers in the supernatural.*

During Mass, right after the simple gifts of bread and wine are presented at the altar, a dialogue ensues. The priest looks at the congregation and says, "Lift up your hearts!" They respond, "We lift them up to the Lord." Then the priest says, "Let us give *thanks* to the Lord our God." The people respond, "It is right and just."

This exchange comes from one of the earliest Christian documents we have regarding worship, called the Didache. This document, *Teaching of the Twelve Apostles,* dates from the late first or early second century.

Its teaching has to do with ethics, church organization, and baptism/Eucharist. It gives a glimpse into how the early church worshipped when they came together to break bread. The roots of the Mass lie in Biblical texts and tradition. In the Didache the early Christian presider would simply say, "Hearts up!"

When it comes to singing or giving thanks, we don't always feel like it. We have to make the decision to elevate our attitudes and lift up our hearts. Eventually, our emotions will catch up to our choices. Gathering with others can help. We can draft in the wake of others at times. At Mass we sing along with the congregation and allow the presider to lead and direct us in our prayer. But sooner or later we will be alone and must choose to lift up our own hearts. There is enough in life to pull our hearts down and make us focus on the negative. Our responsibility is to lift up our hearts several times during our day and give God thanks. It is right, it is just, it is fitting. We hear Paul encourage us,

> Sing psalms and hymns and spiritual songs with thankfulness in your hearts to God. Whatever you do, in word or deed, do everything in the name of the Lord Jesus, giving thanks to God the Father through him. (Col. 3:16-17)

Remember, it is through God's love that we are more than conquerors. Thanksgiving is its own reward. It brings inner serenity and connects us with God's love to elevate us.

Houston, We've had a Problem

Back in 1988 I was a seminarian, and for a year I was assigned at our retreat center in Houston to cut my teeth in ministry. During that apostolic year, I began preaching publicly, learned about ministry, and had a variety of rich experiences. During one of the retreats an engineer from NASA was one of the attendees. He approached me and invited me to come to mission control for a personalized tour. Every young boy growing up wanted to be an astronaut. I jumped at the opportunity. I remember as he showed me around, I saw many things up close. When I entered the mission control room I thought, "This looks so much smaller than it does on TV." While small, it was very complex and advanced technologically, and I marveled when I thought about how much they had accomplished in that room. The engineers, astronauts, and others who work at NASA are people who push the boundaries and literally reach for the stars. I always tell people, "Reach for the stars and at least you'll get the moon." If you don't reach for something, how will you ever get anything?

I thank God for innovators, explorers and adventurers who push limits and boundaries, the status quo, and go beyond the ordinary. Think of where our world is today. We are the first generation of humans who have sent men to the moon! We are able to peer into the depths of our universe and literally look back in time to the very edge of creation through the Hubble telescope. Advanced computers allow us to do things only dreamed of a few years ago. The telecommunications industry has exploded and we can now be connected with news and people on the other side of the world easily and instantaneously. Breakthroughs in the medical world are extending our lives and rendering some diseases obsolete. The ease and speed of modern travel has shrunk our world and brought us closer together.

Creative, daring people in the world of technology, science, medicine and travel are confronting challenges, making new discoveries, and becoming champions in the process. We are the beneficiaries of their innovative and exploratory work. Instead of accepting the status quo, they start from there and go forward. I've heard it said, "Life begins at the end of your comfort zone." Christopher Columbus ventured forth bravely when he was told the world was flat. He discovered new lands and made a way for future generations. Galileo was censured by the Church of his day, but along with others, like Copernicus, courageously proclaimed truths that would revolutionize our thought.

I thank God for adventurers, entrepreneurs, innovators, and explorers. I marvel at artists who express, architects and sculptors who envision, authors and poets who inspire, musicians who elevate us as well as orators who find new ways to motivate. I am grateful for hard-working educators who love their students and find creative ways to convey truths. I am inspired by people who push the boundaries, who reach for more and who don't take no for an answer. They work the problems, face the challenges, and stay determined.

Exploration, adventure, artistry, creativity and advancement are deep within our DNA and part and parcel of our human spirit. God has bestowed upon us a world with infinite possibilities and great potential. It is up to us to "subdue" the earth. (Gen. 1:28) Champions are daring. They reach for the stars and push personal boundaries and limits. They let their imagination run wild and dream dreams. They work hard and believe failure is not an option. We weren't made for less, but for more. You never find out who you really are until you launch into the deep. I love the saying, "Ships in a harbor are safe, but ships were made for the wide open ocean."

My visit to NASA was enriching and made a deep impression on me. I saw what can happen if you dream and push yourself. I was amazed to see what humans can do if we put our minds to it and work together.

I think we all remember what happened to the Apollo 13 mission in April 1970. This mission was popularized by Ron Howard's movie in 1995. Apollo 13 was commanded by three astronauts: James A. Lovell, Jack L. Swigert, and Fred W. Haise. This flight was to be the third landing of humans on the moon. The launch was successful; however, about 200,000 miles away from the earth some exposed wires in an oxygen tank caused a fire and exp' sion, resulting in a crippled ship. The astronauts lost heat, water, and power, as well as the ability to maneuver the ship precisely. They heard the loud bang and thought they struck a meteoroid. It was then that Lovell and Swigert contacted mission control with the famous line, "Houston, we've had a problem."

During the movie the flight controllers at mission control were shown dealing with problem after problem, most of which they had no manual to cover. Every problem demanded a solution that could only be arrived at by thinking outside the box. These problems were urgent and demanded immediate solutions. At one point in the movie, some NASA officials could be seen discussing the crippled ship and thinking the worst. One said, "This could be the worst disaster NASA has ever faced." At that point the lead flight director, Gene Kranz, was shown thinking pensively. He looked at his companions and calmly replied, "With all due respect sir, I believe this is going to be our finest hour."

I have taken this saying to be one of my foundational mottoes. Often when I am approaching a new homily or television series, I'll think, "This is going to be a disaster, what am I going to say that I haven't already said?" I'll fear this is the end for me. The word "disaster" literally means, "when your star falls." I'll then hear, "I've been through this in the past and done well, this is going to be my finest moment!" It is important to encourage yourself in life. You don't always get the supportive words from the crowds, community, or even your spouse. That's when you have to be your own best friend. We read in the Scriptures, "David encouraged himself in the Lord." (1 Sam. 30:6) It's amazing how time after time God will bring something new and fresh out of me. Just when I think I've written and said everything and the well has run dry, some new nugget surfaces. I truly believe that even though I have written nineteen books, produced over 150 television programs, and preached hundreds of different sermons, I've just scratched the surface, because God is in control and continues to bless me.

I recently produced a new television series having the same title as this book, *Challenges Make Champions*. The series contains seven episodes. I've never sold so many DVD's and CD's on television as with this new series. I am convinced as long as I keep applying myself and doing the work, God will keep creating through me and doing something fresh and new. Years ago, when I was on retreat, I was thanking God for the success I was having as a young priest. Then I lamented, "Lord, they like me because I am young. Will like me they when I grow older?" I was quickly reminded of this verse: "They still bring forth fruit in old age, they are *ever* full of sap and green." (Ps. 92:14; italics added) God was telling me the best was yet to come. I believe the same is true in your life, too. Stay planted by the waterside and connected to the vine and you will see abundant fruit.

When you hear that negative voice saying, "This is a disastrous marriage," or, "you're too old," or, "you're too sinful," that is the moment to say, "With all due respect, this is my *finest hour.*" I've adopted this as one of my everyday mottoes, and you can, too.

As you know, six days after the launch, Apollo 13 landed safely in the south Pacific on April 17, 1970. But many problems still had to be solved in order for the safe return to happen. The world watched in tense anticipation as the engineers jerry-rigged a carbon monoxide scrubber where they literally had to figure out how to make a square peg fit into a round hole. They confirmed this truth: necessity is the mother of invention. Also, since they couldn't get back to earth if they turned around immediately, they actually figured out a way to go to the moon and use the gravity of the moon to "catapult" them back to the earth. It worked, and the spacecraft had the thrust it needed to make the return trip to earth.

Remember, the theme of this book is how challenges can catapult you to new levels. Together, the crew and NASA personnel faced every problem and wouldn't take no for an answer. Failure wasn't an option. They found solutions, the entire world cheered their success, and despite the accident and problems, it was NASA's finest hour!

Problems can lead to *promotion*. From the moment we are born we enter a world with problems. A baby may face health problems, familial | *Problems can lead to promotion.* | problems or monetary difficulties through no fault of its own. As we grow older, we must face going to school, and, if you remember, every grade in school has its own set of problems. Besides having to get along with others or encountering the inevitable teacher who doesn't like you, we are all familiar with tests. In order to graduate to the next level or grade you must pass a certain amount of tests. Each exam is replete with problems. It is only when you pass the tests that you can go to the next level. Thus, problems lead to promotion.

I can remember hearing the murmuring of my classmates in high school and college. When we studied trigonometry or calculus I'd hear comments like, "Why in the world must we study this? We will never use any of this in life!" Perhaps, but life does require the problem-solving techniques that we gain by working these particular problems. The value of any education lies in the knowledge we gain by studying various subjects. But the worth of an education lies in the cognitive skills we gain as we face problems. Employers want people with education because it shows they have faced problems and are able to learn, find solutions, and cope with difficulties. Employers want people who are determined, who can think well, and who don't give up easily. Having a degree doesn't guarantee that you are smarter than those who don't, but those who are educated show that they are able to face problems and work through them.

What separates the men from the boys and the women from the girls in life, is not facing problems (we all have to), but working through the problems doggedly and finding solutions. Many get to a certain level of education and then rest on their laurels. When life or a job presents difficulties they don't want the turmoil of trying to figure it out. Others who are more determined are willing to face the work and apply themselves. They are the ones who get the promotion.

Most people aren't willing to take the initiative and continue to educate themselves by reading or deepening their skills. They fall behind and others who are more industrious advance. The truth is, even though you have graduated from school, you are always learning. In order to keep advancing and be promoted you must be ambitious. When in a meeting at work or in your particular community, there will always be problems. Your leaders aren't simply interested in hearing what the problems are—they are interested in solutions. If you want to be a cut above the rest, instead of vocalizing the problems, offer workable solutions.

As you know, I'm an avid golfer. In order to qualify for the professional tour you have to face problems at every level. In golf it is the problems, adversities, and difficulties that separate the professionals from the amateurs. The last and greatest test of your game before advancing to the pro circuit is called Q School. In order to qualify, you have to face stern tests and a variety of hazards. The rough is tough. There are deep bunkers and water hazards, as well as long, narrow holes.

Because golf is an outdoor sport, there are many variables due to the changeable weather. The weather can be very windy, rainy, cold or hot, and a golfer must factor in these conditions over six long rounds. The pressure and problems of the game will identify who is best. At the professional level most players have equal aptitudes; however, when confronted with wind, rain and difficult circumstances, some players lose patience and their ability to perform. True professionals can cope with problems and challenges. In fact, it is the adversities and problems themselves that separate them from the rest and reveal them as the best players in the world. James speaks of this when he writes, "Count it all joy when you meet various trials, for you know that this test produces endurance." (Jas. 1:2-3) It is actually the sufferings in our life that build to character. (Ro. 5:3-4) The truth about trouble is that it teases out talent. In this respect, problems make professionals.

Problems also produce *pronouncements*. Some fifty years ago, the Catholic Church called the Second Vatican Council. These sessions were stretched out over a few years. The Church fathers concentrated on how the church is seen by and related to the modern world. Their dogmatic pronouncements led to sweeping changes. Many in the pews struggled with these changes and murmured, "Why did the Church have to change now? I was happy with the Church the way it was." Scores of priests and nuns left religious life. Some got married. Laity wrestled with the changes in the liturgy and what Catholicism was becoming.

What most don't understand is that Vatican II was the twenty-first Ecumenical council in the history of the church. Every time there is a council, there are changes and new decrees. The Church is never stagnant, but always fluid. It's not that the Church doesn't have the truth—we have the fullness of truth. But, as the people of God on pilgrimage, we are trying to grasp more fully the revelation given to us by God. Like any living being, we learn, grow, and change over time. Truths don't change and are always absolute, but our understanding of these truths is what causes us to adapt.

Unlike previous councils, the Second Vatican Council was unique in that it didn't declare any anathemas or settle any grave heresies. In the Bible we read about the first Church Council in Jerusalem. In chapter fifteen of the Acts of the Apostles, the apostles and elders met for what has been called the controversy over the admission of the Gentiles. The first Christians were Jewish Christians. In time, through successful evangelization efforts, non-Jews were starting to believe in Jesus. This was a wonderful development but led to many questions. Should the Gentiles be circumcised? What other laws must they observe? When the apostles and elders met over this problem, they came to a ground-breaking formulation: "We believe we shall be saved through the grace of the Lord Jesus, just as they will." (Acts 15:11) In other words, salvation comes through grace, not by works of the Jewish law. The apostles came to the revolutionary decision not to lay the heavy burdens of the law upon new Christians. This opened the door for multitudes of people to come into the church and would eventually lead to a break from its traditionally Jewish beginnings.

Another pronouncement came at the Council of Nicaea in 325. The Arian heresy proclaimed Jesus was not fully divine. The fathers of Nicaea refuted this heresy and stated Jesus was of one nature and substance (consubstantial) with God the Father. Our present-day creed came from this council.

In the Council of Ephesus in 451, the Catholic dogma was defined that the Blessed Virgin is the mother of God giving birth to Jesus who had two natures, thus refuting the heresy of Nestorius, the Archbishop of Constantinople. Many other Councils were called throughout the ages, refuting heresies and developing doctrines. Most of these councils were called precisely because of problems and difficulties people had with doctrine and church law. While they may seem bad in and of themselves, problems can produce pronouncements.

Problems can also produce prophets. Elijah lived at a time of great idolatry in Israel. There had been a succession of evil kings, and Ahab married the Phoenician Jezebel, who swayed his heart to worship her god, Baal. They were also undergoing a devastating drought. I remember visiting Mt. Carmel in Israel and there is a statue of the bearded prophet Elijah holding a sword aloft and slaying a priest of Baal. If you remember, Elijah challenged 450 priests of the god Baal and 400 prophets of Asherah to a contest. Each side made sacrifices to their God. The God who was the strongest was to light the sacrifice through a supernatural act. Elijah mocked the priests of Baal as they danced and cut themselves while calling upon their god. When it was Elijah's turn, he had them pour water on the sacrifice three times, filling the trenches all around. Suddenly, fire from heaven came, consuming the sacrifice and thus declaring the God of Israel the one true God, and vindicating Elijah as his prophet. The prophets of Baal were all slain. God further attested to Elijah by ending the drought. (1 Kings 18:20-46)

Prophets may be attested to by supernatural acts or have astounding visions such as Isaiah or Ezekiel did. They may even predict the future, as most have. However, the true definition of a prophet is one who speaks for God. Nehemiah was a court officer in the Persian court. Jerusalem had been destroyed, the temple demolished in 586 B.C., and the walls torn down by the Babylonians when they took the Hebrews captive into exile. Years later, the temple was rebuilt under the leadership and direction of the prophets Haggai and Zechariah. The walls were necessary to protect the city. While the people were slack in repairing the breached walls, Nehemiah was the catalyst for them to begin again and they finished the project in a mere fifty-two days.

Nehemiah, Haggai and Zechariah were men who were raised up to speak for God when the problems of rebuilding the temple and protecting the holy city arose. Jesus, too, was called a prophet when he spoke for God and announced God's Kingdom. He addressed the problems of injustice and reached out to the marginalized. The problems of poverty and inequality promoted by an oppressive Roman government were addressed by Jesus throughout his ministry. Jesus' prophetic ministry was one of setting the captives free. The problems of humanity led to God sending us the greatest of all prophets, his very own Son.

Adversity, danger, and problems are exactly what the early church faced. The civil and religious authorities did everything they could to squash this newborn movement initially called "the Way." (Acts 9:2) The apostles were threatened, imprisoned and even put to death for their faith in Jesus Christ. Yet, God worked with them and through them. He filled them with the boldness of the Holy Spirit. God made a way for the Church when there was no way.

We face many problems in the church today. One major problem is a diminishment in vocations to religious life. Our community was rocked by the sexual abuse scandal; we deliberate, trying to determine how to handle gays and same sex marriages; many parishes are in the process of merging; religious congregations are dying; conservatives and liberals struggle to see eye to eye; there are financial problems. Yet all of these pale in comparison to the problems the early church faced.

Christianity was almost crushed before it ever gained any momentum. The number one problem the early Church faced was persecution. There was a high cost to following Christ. Christians were being imprisoned and murdered because of their faith in Jesus, and many were hunted down simply because they were believers.

When I was in the seminary we were taught about a principle that was eye-opening to me. This truth was highlighted in the Acts of the Apostles.

When Stephen was put to death, a great persecution arose against the church in Jerusalem; and *they were all scattered* throughout the region of Judea and Samaria...and those who were scattered went about preaching the word.

(Acts 8:1,4; italics added)

Just when the early church was in danger of dying out, it became their finest moment. Persecution led to proclamation! Instead of being squelched they were scattered. Picture little white dandelion seeds blown by the wind everywhere. What is the profound truth Acts 8 proclaims? The harshest, greatest problem the church has ever faced led to its growth! We've all heard the saying, "The blood of martyrs is the seed of new Christians." Whenever evil comes against the body of Christ, it is evil itself that is thwarted. As the Pharisee Gamaliel said, "If this undertaking is of God, you will not be able to overthrow them." (Acts 5:39)

The same can be said for individuals in the grip of addiction. Often they are in denial and live rationalizing and justifying their dysfunctional behavior in their own minds. People can be adept at lying to themselves. This deception will go on for a while until a problem develops. The problem may be a bottoming-out experience. It could be an accident, being violent toward a loved one, or having a blackout where nothing from the previous night is remembered. Or, the problem could take the form of a gathering of friends and relatives conducting an intervention on the addicted person in order to get them to admit their behavior. In an intervention several people confront the person with their dysfunctional behavior.

The intervention usually results in the person admitting their addiction. It is the shock and embarrassment of the intervention that can lead to positive change.

One of my friends who used to be a coach has a website with many motivational sayings. On the bottom of his emails he has this quote, "When the pain of where you are is greater than the pain of where you need to be, then you will move." Often pain, and sometimes guilt, is the great motivator. It was for the prodigal son. He woke up and moved only after he suffered.

I've heard it said that when it is time to kick the young eaglet out of the nest, the mother eagle makes it hard for him. She covers the nest with thorns and makes it painful for the young eagle to stay. Before long, the young eagle gets the message and moves.

Most ministers preach, "let go of the guilt," and I do, too. It isn't good to hold on to guilt from the past. It can weigh us down. Yet guilt is a gift given to us by God. Guilt from wrongdoing is an indicator something is amiss. We must pay attention to the guilt in our life and let it serve its purpose. The pain of guilt can motivate us to change our ways. It can be a deterrent to further wrongdoing. We need to let it go, but not before it serves its purpose. Yes, lay your burden down, but only after your burden lifts you up.

Lay your burden down, but only after your burden lifts you up.

I like to tell the story of the monk and the atheist who were walking and discussing life after death. As they walked, storm clouds gathered and it began getting very cold. A blizzard was approaching. As they talked, the monk said there would be a resurrection while the atheist couldn't see how that could possibly happen. It began to snow heavily, and since they were miles from camp, they quickly turned around. Before long they came upon a man who had fallen and broken his leg and couldn't walk. Because of the blizzard the atheist walked right on by. The monk bent over and took his arm and carried him on his back. It was difficult, and the weight slowed him down. The storm continued ferociously.

An hour later, as the monk trudged through the snow with the man clinging to him, he suddenly bumped into something beneath the snow that almost made him fall. It was the atheist. The frigid cold and ferocity of the storm were too much for him. He had fallen on the trail, where he froze to death. The priest, however, was sweating. The weight of his burden kept him alive in the cold and snow. Similarly, our burdens can be our blessings.

Many people like to work puzzles. I can remember seeing a 5,000-piece puzzle scattered on a table one time and feeling so intimidated by it all. I thought, "Where would you begin on something like this? Putting this puzzle together is impossible!" Actually, if you look at the picture on the cover and start where you can find an edge or some easy shape or similar colors, you have an easier start to the puzzle. Little by little, piece by piece, you do what is possible and eventually the impossible falls into place.

That's exactly the thought process I had when I began writing books. When I began writing my first book in 1999, I was very intimidated by the thought of it and feared I wouldn't be able to finish the project. I kept thinking of Jesus' words, "For if you lay the foundation and are not able to finish they will ridicule you." (Lk 14:29) I was afraid those in my community would know I was starting to write and if I abandoned the project they would talk about me. Because I was afraid of this, I hardly told anyone I was writing the book. Writing a 200-plus page book was a daunting task and I did feel overwhelmed. But I began, and persevered by remembering something I did in the seminary.

At the end of our four-year theology training, each student must produce his or her mission statement. This 100-plus page document is our statement of theology, Christology, ecclesiology, and mission. We have to submit this document to a panel of three teachers to be judged for comprehensiveness and orthodoxy. After their reading and evaluation of this treatise, a determination would be made about our graduation. Naturally, I was nervous about their finding, but even more stressed about writing the document itself. I had written twenty-to-thirty page papers in the past, but never anything this long and varied in its scope. There were a number of details and subjects I was required to cover. My professors wanted to know what I learned over the years and what my stance on Church issues was. I trusted I was in line with Church teaching, but the length and cohesiveness of this document bothered me. I worked for months on the paper, all the while finishing up my final semester of classes.

I was able to author a 125-page document that covered the necessary requirements and more. I was actually amazed at what came out of me when I sat down, applied myself, and wrote. When my teachers evaluated my statement and discussed it with me, much to my delight, I passed with flying colors. I graduated with a Master of Divinity degree with a specialization in the Scriptures. I was ordained a deacon shortly thereafter and then a priest nine months later. This document defined my seminary experience and paved the way for my future ministry.

I never forgot this problem from my seminary days. That long document actually became a catalyst that would help me when I contemplated the huge task of writing a book. I knew that I had written that mission statement with creativity and orthodoxy. Although it was long, when I applied myself I found I was writing things I didn't know I had in me. I thought, "If I was able to be successful when faced with that challenge, then I believe I can write a book." Success with that problem long ago gave me the confidence to try this new endeavor. Although the book would be longer and scrutinized by many more people, I believed I could do it. In 1999,

> *You don't know who you really are or what you can possibly do until you are faced with a problem.*

I began writing *Live Passionately!* and now, fifteen years later, this is my nineteenth book! Because the sales and royalties of my books lead to the monies I need to produce and air television programs, my problem has led to the promotion of the Gospel as well as my own personal advancement.

You don't know who you really are or what you can possibly do until you are faced with a problem.

MOJO

Our community does our banking with a bank that has a slogan: *The bank with momentum.* Momentum is crucial in sports. In golf you can be struggling, then suddenly a birdie will change the momentum for the better. In football games you can see which team has the momentum. It seems like the fumbles and interceptions go their way. When I work out on the elliptical, the first step is always the hardest. Once you get the machine moving, you create a flow that is sustainable. When I swim in a pool, the motion creates a flow of movement. If I stop, it is that much harder to get moving again. Have you ever seen good swimmers when they get to the end of the pool? Instead of stopping, they somersault and push off the end of the pool, keeping the momentum going.

As I mentioned before, I recently lost 18 pounds. It didn't happen overnight. It took a year of working out and eating right. Weight loss has a lot to do with momentum. Once you start losing, if you stop exercising or eat too much, it brings the lifestyle flow to a halt.

Momentum is key in ministry also. As I write books, preach, or create and produce new programs for television, a wonderful momentum has developed. Creativity has become a lifestyle of discipline and determination. All the areas I invest in feed into each other and bring growth. It is like a snowball that keeps rolling and grows larger and larger as time goes on.

It is important in life to create momentum. Once you have momentum in your life, ministry or business takes on a life of its own. It is similar to a pendulum. Unless there is an energy or force applied it remains still. But once it starts moving, the pendulum has a momentum of its own. Or, it is like the snowball effect. Once the snowball is rolled in sticky snow, it keeps growing and growing. Apply the energy you need in life to get the ball rolling, to make the pendulum swing. Then keep doing what you did to get the ball rolling in the first place. Your drive and determination will take you places you never thought you could go.

Problems in life demand solutions. In many ways, as we journey through life, we are like jugglers. We may have many balls in the air at the same time and we have to handle all of them, one at a time. Each of those balls is a problem and each one demands attention and a solution. I have become adept at juggling. I've found I can do it if I focus on one thing then shift my attention to the next.

I've noticed that most people in life like to talk about their problems, but few are willing to work on a solution. If you want to rise above the rest in your business or community, acknowledge the problems and find solutions. Don't just accept things the way they are. Bosses love it when you take the initiative and address problems creatively. Think outside the box.

I was in a grocery store at the deli counter once. They offer to make deli sandwiches to order. When I saw the ingredients I noticed they had whitish green lettuce and no spinach. I'm into health and the nutritional value of whitish lettuce is not much. I said to the young girl, "You ought to have green leafy spinach to offer. People would love it." She kind of shrugged it off. Then I said, "I'm serious. Tell your manager about it. He would love a suggestion like that and it would probably lead to your promotion."

I noticed some time later that spinach was being offered as an ingredient and the lettuce was not available anymore. It wasn't just in that store, but in the whole chain of stores. I never saw that young girl again. I'm thinking it was because she got promoted to another level.

Politicians have to deal with problems of every sort. The best are those who come up with workable solutions. Doctors and pharmaceuticals are all about addressing health problems with proper diagnosis, treatment, and medication. Relationship problems abound and therapists and counselors are called upon to find solutions. Every day, businesses are faced with problems that demand answers.

Wake Up the World!

Religious life is an area where there are many problems. As I write this we are in a special year of "consecrated life" in our Catholic church. This unique year is meant to recognize the many religious priests, sisters, and brothers, and the fine ministries all are doing. But Pope Francis designated this special year to call attention to the vocation crisis in the hope that more people will become aware of religious life and generously join our communities. The theme of the year of consecrated life is "Wake up the World!"

Every four years, my Passionist Community of Holy Cross province has what is called a "chapter." During a chapter the sixty of us who are members of the province gather with our dedicated laity to celebrate our life and history and address any problems we face. The outcome of these chapters is new leadership, pronouncements, and legislation. Complications we are dealing with now have to do with diminishment, aging, finances, and a very uncertain future. Religious communities across the globe are dying out. Their original reasons for coming together are still valid, but the vocations are few. Every chapter we meet, discuss, and strive to find solutions.

One of the areas that is very critical is our finances. Because we are diminishing and our work force is aging, our income has gone down steadily. This problem demanded attention and together we came up with a solution. We decided to engage in a capital campaign. The monies raised from this campaign would benefit our elderly religious and help to educate laity. So far, this solution is working. Through hard work and generous benefactors we have been able to meet our needs so far, and we thank God for these blessings.

Another severe problem is diminishment. Our priests and brothers are growing older and many can no longer minister. One wonderful solution has been to empower laity to take more of a leadership role in the community. Many of our retreat centers have Passionists as spiritual leaders, but laity run the administrative side of the center. Some lay people even preach on the retreat and mission teams. We try to instill our Passionist charism (gift) into all of our employees and help them to see they don't just work for us but are part of our mission. Our challenges are ongoing, but we gather to identify and address each problem with solutions. In problem solving, it is necessary to name the predicament but not get stuck there. We must work on viable solutions for the sake of our mission. The Passionists' mission is to proclaim the passion of Jesus to the world.

The Bible is full of problems. Certainly, the greatest difficulty that emerges from its pages comes from its first book, Genesis. Adam and Eve sinned and fell from God. They experienced guilt, shame and separation from God. Thus, death came to human beings. This story tells us that all humanity fell and, as a result, we die. How would God remedy this? What would be the solution? In Genesis 3:15 we hear God promise, "The seed of the woman will bruise your head and you (the serpent) shall bruise his heel." This has always been interpreted as the foretelling of the Messiah to come who would crush the head of the serpent while the serpent strikes at his foot. In other words, God's anointed one would suffer, but his suffering would bring victory.

God's solution to the mess of fallen humanity is Jesus. Jesus is God's solution to the greatest problem humanity has ever faced: death. God turned sin and death inside out.

At the Easter Vigil the deacon sings the Exsultet. This hymn of praise lauds God for his wonderful works. I love the verse, "O Happy fault, that earned for us so great, so glorious a Redeemer!" It was precisely our *fall*—our *fault*—that led to resurrection.

All of us face adversities, challenges, and disabilities. We all have hurdles to jump and mountains to climb. To be human is to face problems. We are confronted by physical suffering, relationship problems, addiction, and broken dreams. Everyone's got something to deal with, and most of us have more than one thing. Yet, suffering leads to character. God uses the difficulties of life to elevate us.

> *God uses the difficulties of life to elevate us.*

This book proclaims not only the reality of afflictions and difficulties, but a wonderful twist: it is the challenges that can make us champions. Our problems and hardships can promote us and bring us to growth and new wisdom. I am hoping you will look at your life situation and circumstances in new ways, gaining a new perspective. When a person uses a trampoline they temporarily go down, but the further down they go, the higher it catapults them up. Don't allow your particular hardships to bring you down, but lift you up.

Think for a moment about some of the numerous examples I have given you in this chapter. I've written about a blind and deaf woman writing twelve books. I've talked about a woman with no legs dancing with the stars. I've shared about a crippled ship using the gravity of the moon to take it home. I now minister on television when originally I had no money or contacts. These are extreme examples meant to demonstrate that if these people could do it, certainly you can, too. We do it, not in our own strength, but through God's love. It is God who energizes us and anoints us with the creativity and determination to face our problems and be uplifted. Along the way, we gain character as our virtues are tested.

In 1996 the summer Olympics were held in Atlanta, Georgia. The games were a wonderful display of the talent and ability of athletes from around the world. Pop singer Gloria Estefan was chosen to create a song that would become the theme of that Olympic games. The song she sang was called *Reach*, and it spoke of dreams, doing whatever it takes, being strong, putting it all on the line and touching the sky. The video shows the Olympic flame, runners straining, basketball players dunking, pole-vaulters clearing, and divers diving with perfection. In the end, a gold medal was placed upon a champion who faced adversities, displayed courage, and put their spirit to the test.

I conclude one of my talks during my missions by having everyone do something symbolic. First I have them stand. I then ask them to reach their hands as high as they can (You can see an example of this on the top of my page on www.frcedric.org). They all look like they are praising God. Actually, when you push the boundaries of your life, you *are* praising God. When they are standing with their arms aloft, I then say, "Reach! Reach higher! Reach for the stars and at least you will get the moon!" (see page 1.) I invite you to stand up to your problems and challenges and reach. Don't let your sufferings, disabilities, and problems overwhelm you. Let them promote you! Don't let them diminish you, let them challenge you to go higher. Don't give up, *go* up. Life isn't meant to defeat you but to catapult you to new heights. You have great potential and possibility. Who you are is God's gift to you. Who you *become* is your gift to God.

3
THE CHALLENGE OF FREEDOM

One of the places I hate to go is a pet store. It's not because I dislike pets—I love them. But it breaks my heart to see animals and birds in cages. Dogs were meant to run. Cats were created to roam. Birds are designed to fly and fish were meant to swim in the open. It is so sad to see their freedom taken away when they are captive. When I go into a pet store I want to adopt them all, but I know I can't.

Years ago I saw the movie *Born Free*. It is a tear-jerking movie about a lion cub, Elsa, who was adopted by a family. The family adopted the cub and kept her in their home. When it was time for them to give the cub up to the zoo, they decided to keep her. Eventually, they domesticated Elsa and when she grew up, they taught her how to live in the wild. When Elsa was finally ready they brought their beloved pet to the wild and let her go. She was meant to be free because she was born free.

If animals are born free, how much more free are humans? Besides the gift of life itself, the first gift given to us by God was free will. We have the power to choose, to decide. We are responsible for our own choices and should not be forced or coerced by anyone else. Yet, while we were born free, multitudes are in bondage. The slavery occurred, not so much because someone forced them into it, but because they were lured into captivity.

I have seen this captivity first hand. I've been a priest for many years and people come to me for confession and counseling who are trapped in many areas. Some are stuck in addictions to alcohol, painkillers, sex, the internet, gambling, food, or shopping. In many ways, we are hard-wired for addiction and we must be vigilant lest we allow ourselves to become slaves to substances and behaviors.

We are creatures of habit. I have a set routine in the morning. It makes me feel comfortable, works for me, and I find that even when I travel I keep my routine on the road. My surroundings may change, but I have developed a pattern that works. This patterned practice helps me to stay focused. Why keep reinventing the wheel?

Professional golfers develop a personalized pre-shot routine. This manner of getting ready to hit the shot varies from player to player but is extremely important. Developing and keeping the same routine is crucial, especially when there is pressure or adversity in the round. There is refuge in the routine.

While routines can help us, they can ruin us as well. It is easy to develop habits of watching too much television or surfing the internet. What begins as curiosity or relaxation can quickly turn into an ingrained habit. Once we have that repetitive habit we don't feel comfortable without it. We can develop habits of texting, watching television excessively, overeating, smoking, and speeding while driving. Actually, there is an endless variety of detrimental habits we can slip into. The dictionary defines a habit as a regular, settled tendency that is hard to give up. When a habit becomes unmanageable it crosses over into the category of slavery.

A military strategist once told me, "Even your enemies are creatures of habit." The best way to gain victory over them is to know their repetitive tendencies and exploit them. Our enemy, Satan, strategizes against us in this way too. He knows our weak points and tries to gain victory over us through them.

We all have both good habits and bad habits. I've found the best way to break a bad habit is to replace it with a good habit. For example, instead of watching game shows after the evening news, try reading. Once you make this shift on a regular basis, then the bad habit has been overcome by cultivating a new, better habit. Adopting the new habit pushes out the old. You have to intentionally make better choices to begin good habits. It is the same with your thoughts. Instead of trying to stop negative thinking, simply replace the bad thoughts with positive thoughts. You can't think two things at one time. This is something I tell myself all the time. When I start worrying and making a negative list, I tell myself, "Cedric, focus on the positive." As I focus on being optimistic, the positive pushes out the negative.

Besides bad habits, people can be trapped in emotional quicksand such as guilt, shame, self-condemnation, and self-rejection. These emotions can arise from traumatic experiences or as a result of unwanted behaviors. Not all guilt is bad, but it can be easy to become addicted to negative feelings that lead to self-loathing.

In addition, many are oppressed by anger, resentment, and non-forgiveness. We all have relationships in our lives that are messy and out of control. It is easy to be touchy and easily offended. If you are overly-sensitive you are setting yourself up for disaster. Someone may inadvertently cut you off on the road and you let it spoil your day. I've heard it said if you won't forgive others it is like drinking poison and thinking it will hurt another person. Bitterness is a self-imposed prison.

Also, multitudes are bound by fear, negative thoughts and attitudes, worry, doubts, and anxiety. It's easy to think the worst. Murphy's law becomes their rule. I hear so many say, "Just my luck. This always happens to me. I never get any breaks." In some ways, when you are afraid and negative, you can actually attract bad things to your life. Job said, "What I feared has come upon me, what I dreaded has happened to me." (Job 3:25)

Most of these bondages are self-imposed. No one forced these on us. We allowed them, were tempted into them and they quickly flourished. We nebulously choose them over and over again with our own free will. Sadly, our freedom can lead to slavery. That is why we put age limits preventing children from drinking, smoking or viewing adult sites online. These things are highly addictive and children aren't able to fully reason yet.

Is there an area where you are in slavery and not free? The first step to freedom is to be rigorously honest with yourself. You must identify and admit the area(s) where you are stuck. Take a moment now and think about where you might be bound. Use the previous page where I talk about addictions, habits, thoughts, emotions, behaviors, and attitudes to guide you in your reflection. This first step is crucial. Unless you admit you have a problem in a certain area, you will never experience freedom. The first step in the AA program is when a person admits they are powerless over the substance of alcohol. Similarly, we must acknowledge our areas of bondage as well as our powerlessness over them.

All things are possible with God.

The important second step of AA says, "We came to believe that a power greater than ourselves could restore us to sanity." I love what Jesus said in John 8:36, "If therefore the Son shall make you free, you shall be free indeed." We may be responsible for our own slavery, but there is a way out. Jesus came to bring us freedom. In Jesus there is power, ability, and a new desire to be free. He can do for us everything we cannot do for ourselves. *All things are possible* with God.

Freedom is Jesus' job description. In his inaugural sermon in Luke, the Gospel writer tells us why Jesus came.

The Spirit of the Lord is upon me, because he has anointed me to preach good news to the poor. He has sent me to *proclaim release to the captives* and recovering of sight to the blind, *to set at liberty those who are oppressed,* to proclaim the acceptable year of the Lord.

(Lk. 4:18-19; italics added)

I had this Scripture proclaimed at my ordination to the priesthood because I believe the ministry of a priest is to proclaim release and set at liberty those who are oppressed. We priests are continuing in our lives the ministry of Jesus Christ himself. Jesus touched and helped people everywhere. People who were bound by demons, fear, anger, sickness, and even death, were healed and liberated. Jesus has the power to overcome any bondage. He can heal you everywhere you hurt and feel stuck.

Adam/Eve, Where are you?

In my ministry I meet people who are in one of three places (actually, the same person can be in each of the three places at the same time). The first place is feeling stuck or enslaved. It could be they are mired in anger or a bad habit of some sort. Possibly they feel they are in a desert spiritually. I hear people talk all the time about feeling like they are just going through the motions at Mass. They are devoid of consolation in their prayer life. They try to get quiet and end up distracted and don't feel like God is speaking or answering their prayers.

Others feel like they are going backwards and that their addiction is getting worse. Instead of forgiving the one who hurt them, bitterness and resentment overwhelm them even more. Rather than being courageous, people succumb to fear. Laziness and lack of discipline have led to unfulfilled dreams.

Still others talk about *growth, movement forward, and progression*. They tell me they are moving in the Lord and making progress. They are aggressively pursuing their passion. Some are replacing bad habits with good ones. As I said, one person may be in all three places at the same time. You may be stuck in fear, going backwards in an addiction, yet able to forgive those who hurt you.

Freedom means movement, momentum and consistency in all of your areas. Freedom doesn't mean you are perfect, but heading toward perfection. The Hebrews received an initial encounter with freedom when they passed through the Red Sea. But it was their journey of forty years that led them to the Promised Land. Similarly, we may encounter our "Red Sea" moments. But then we must journey responsibly toward our goal.

As you encounter freedom in one area, other areas where you are still enslaved will catch up. If your life is a mess in several areas, start with cleaning your house. Once you begin movement in one area, you can start to gain authority in other areas. Momentum is comprehensive and leads to the snowball effect.

We were made for freedom. Being free from the shackles of oppression is in our blood. Deep in our DNA

God put the longing for freedom within us. Liberty is in our genes. We instinctively resist having to live with any type of domination. This quest began with free will and continues with the deep desire not to be enslaved to anything or anyone.

The ideal of freedom attracts us and calls out to us. We instinctively know there is a way of life that is liberating, enriching, and fulfilling. We know we were made for independence. With freedom comes inner peace and joy. The day a person is released from prison they are ecstatic with joy. Similarly, we were made to experience the fruit of freedom.

In order to obey the challenge of freedom we must be willing to change our lifestyle to find a better way. We are responsible for our own freedom. God will help us, but we must be aggressive. We are free agents, morally, and God will woo us but never force us into the best life we can have. The discrepancy between where we are now and where we could be is a great challenge. But challenges make champions. We can overcome the pull of our fallen nature and enjoy the glorious freedom of the children of God. We are people of dignity and ultimate worth, sons and daughters of the Most High God.

The Challenge to Improve

One of the great appeals of golf is the challenge to get better. When I first started playing I wasn't very good, but every once in a while I'd hit a great shot. I'd think, "Why can't I do that all the time? I have it in me." But I was very inconsistent. As I practiced and worked on my game I would hit good shots more frequently. I progressed to a three handicap, my best ever. I discovered that everyone can hit good shots, but few can do it consistently. Tiger Woods was the number one golfer in the world for years.

Even though he had won many majors, as well as a variety of other tournaments, he changed swing coaches. He aggressively pursued another swing and even changed his equipment. Most adhere to the philosophy, "If it ain't broke, don't fix it." He was number one in the world! Why change? When asked about the changes he said, "I want to keep getting better."

Consistency is key, whether it be in sports, morality, your professional life, or your spiritual life. Faithfulness means doing what is right over and over and over. Most times you won't feel like it and no one will applaud you. Often we perform upright deeds but they are mixed in with sinful ones or bad habits. James asks, "Can fresh water and brackish flow from the same spring?" (3:11) He is warning us to live with consistency. The Christian walk is about becoming more and more consistent in every area of our lives.

When driving down the street we often see the word "School" painted on the blacktop—a warning to slow down. As we journey in life we are all going to school. Life is about learning, growing and the challenge to become better and realize our potential. I saw a bumper sticker once that said, "The truly educated person never stops going to school." This is a statement that rings true.

While it may not be formal education, life is about learning. In religious life and the priesthood we call this "ongoing formation." It is important that we read, educate ourselves, and attend retreats and workshops in order to stay on top of advancements and developments. Similarly, I've read that if you aren't staying up on the new developments in your field you will get run over by the people who are. Professionally, it is important that you stay aware of new advances. In the area of health, be aware of your condition. See your doctor and do what it takes to have the best health you can. Listen to your body.

In the midst of writing this book, I made the tough decision to retire from golf. I love the sport and have played for over forty-three years. However, it was taking a toll on my body. In recent years I had to have a partial right knee replacement, my discs are degenerating, and I had sciatica and back pain. My shoulder, neck, and hip hurt after playing. I finally listened to my body and made a very difficult decision. No more golf. What made the decision hard is people still invite me out and I have dozens and dozens of new balls I've never used. It took me a while to finally come to this decision.

I haven't given up recreation, though. I have replaced a harmful habit with a better one. I now work out every day when I am home. I have lost weight, and most of all, I don't hurt anymore. Listening to my body forced me to make better choices.

Paul and Freedom

Paul the apostle reflected about freedom in a number of his letters. His letter to the Galatians has been called the Magna Carta of Christian liberty. In this epistle we read Paul's famous statement, "For freedom Christ has set us free." (Gal. 5:1) Paul was referring to freedom from trying to be right with God through the keeping of the Mosaic law. Rather, it is through our faith in Jesus that we are justified. Our glory is the cross of Jesus which saves us. Jesus has set us free from the law, free from sin and free from death. Freedom is the gift of grace.

Our glory is the cross of Jesus which saves us.

In Paul's letter to the Romans, he talks about the "glorious liberty of the children of God." (Ro. 8:21) This liberty is a freedom of being indwelt, led and guided by God's Holy Spirit. The Spirit helps us to put to death the deeds of the flesh and leads us into works that are pleasing to God. Rather than being dominated by ordinary impulses and feelings, we are led by the person of God into the fullness of freedom. Even our prayer life is renewed because the Spirit helps us and intercedes for us according to the will of God.

> For all who are led by the Spirit of God are sons and daughters of God. For you did not receive the spirit of slavery to fall back into fear, but you have received the spirit of sonship. (Ro. 8:14-15)

When Paul reflected about freedom, he even talked about creation itself. Most people accept that we are presently in the midst of climate change. The polar caps are melting and the seas are rising. The majority of scientists are foretelling catastrophic consequences for our planet due to the greenhouse effect and pollution. Air, water and noise pollution are having a detrimental effect on our earth. Our rainforests are disappearing and animals are being affected; our oceans are being depleted of edible fish; some are hunting protected animals and whales that may become extinct. When we Passionists reflect about the passion of Christ, we include the "contemporary" passion. The contemporary passion refers to Christ's sufferings today in the poor, the hungry, and those who suffer great injustice.

In our reflections on the contemporary passion, we also include the passion of the Earth itself. Most use its resources and don't reflect on the great damage we are leaving in our wake. One of our priests, Fr. Joe Mitchell, C.P., has dedicated himself to proclaiming how we can care for the earth. He teaches about the passion of the earth. The earth is becoming toxic in its waters; its air is becoming polluted; its forests are being depleted; the fertility of its soil is being diminished; it's becoming desolate in the loss of species; and it is threatened with nuclear waste with no reliable means of disposal. Fr. Mitchell has founded the Earth and Spirit Center behind our monastery in Louisville, Ky. Another of our priests, the late Fr. Thomas Berry, C.P., taught, "The future can exist only when we understand the universe as composed of subjects to be communed with, not as objects to be exploited." [2]

Paul talked about our planet's decay and imperfect state as bondage. Think of the destructive hurricanes, ferocious tornadoes and devastating earthquakes and consider the tsunamis, floods and droughts that plague our planet. Remember, there is a lack of food and water for multitudes. Reflect on the inhospitable environments of hot and cold some must live in. Remember how multitudes of birds and animals suffer every day. Paul wrote that God subjected our environment to futility but not without hope. Then he made the magnificent statement, "Creation itself will be set free from its bondage to decay and obtain the glorious liberty of the children of God." (Ro. 8:21)

Even creation longs for liberty!

Freedom from Sin

In John 8:36 we hear Jesus teach, "If the Son makes you free, you will be free indeed." Earlier he had taught that if you know the truth, the truth will make you free. Knowing Jesus and following his teachings leads to freedom. In

2 For more information on Fr. Joe's ministry visit
  www.earthandspiritcenter.org

this particular case, Jesus was talking about freedom from sin. The Bible has a keen interest in sin. Every book has sin and our obedience as one of its main themes. The book of Ecclesiastes says it well as it concludes:

> The end of the matter: all has been heard. Fear God, and keep his commandments; for this is the whole duty of all humans. For God will bring every deed into judgment, with every secret thing, whether good or evil. (Ec. 12:13-14)

Sin literally means to "miss the mark." Sin is transgressing God's will for your life and disobedience to God's ways. Sin is violating our own well-formed conscience. There are also sins of omission when we don't do what we should do. We become slaves to sin when we commit sin or don't do what we know we should do. Whichever we choose becomes our master, either Christ or sin. Paul called himself a slave of Christ. The Bible reveals we are all slaves to something; we either serve God or sin. Serving sin leads to bondage, serving God to freedom. Jesus offers us the grace and power to live morally upright lives, and walk in liberty as children of God.

The Bible reveals we are all slaves to something...

The artist and sculptor Michelangelo created many famous works of art. I had the privilege of seeing many of his works in Rome and at the Accademia Gallery in Florence. The Accademia houses works such as Michelangelo's David. I was struck also by some of his lesser-known works called "The Prisoners," or "The Slaves." While there are four such pieces, the one called "The Awakening Slave" is very poignant. They are all unfinished works. You can see the person coming out of the block of marble surrounded and encapsulated by the unfinished stone. In the Awakening Slave the figure is shown to be writhing and straining, wanting desperately to escape. Yet he is still held captive. So it is with sin. We have been set free, yet we wrestle and struggle to receive our freedom from this captivity.

The US: A Free Country

Years ago my dad had a U.S. flag he used to proudly display on Flag Day or other national holidays. Dad served the US in World War II and was honorably discharged from the Navy as a disabled veteran. Our flag is a symbol of the freedom we enjoy in our country.

Before most sporting events we sing, *The Star Spangled Banner*. This song, our national anthem, was composed by Francis Scott Key in 1812. In the song we sing, "Oh, say does that star spangled banner yet wave o'er the land of the free and the home of the brave?" We salute or put our hands over our hearts as we sing, thus showing honor and respect to the flag.

In addition to allegiance to our flag, we are singing of our freedom and the brave who won it and those who preserve it for us. Today, some people ride with flags outside of their car or place bumper stickers bearing the flag on their car or truck. I saw one sticker of the flag on a Marine's pick-up truck that read: "These colors don't run." This refers to the patriotism and bravery symbolized by the flag.

We call our flag "Old Glory." When the wind blows through it there is a manifestation of the waves of glory that God gives those who are truly free.

The United States is a free country. We are all familiar with the Declaration of Independence. In the preamble to this foundational document we read these truths to be self-evident: "life, liberty, and the pursuit of happiness." These three unalienable rights have been given to all by our creator and for which governments are created to protect. In our Constitution we read about the blessings of liberty. This legally-binding document contains the Bill of Rights, which proclaims freedom after freedom. In the amendments to our Constitution we hear about the freedom of press, speech, religion, and so many other freedoms we treasure today.

As I said before, I grew up in Massachusetts, which is one of the original thirteen colonies that rebelled against the tyranny of England. Our history and the quest for freedom was a part of our culture. The desire for freedom was ingrained in us. I learned about Paul Revere, his courageous horseback ride and "one if by land, two if by sea" when I was very little. I've walked the Freedom Trail in Boston and visited the Old North Church, the Bunker Hill monument, and Faneuil Hall. I've been to Lexington and Concord, where battles were fought. I've seen the old tombstones of those who fought and died for freedom, and I've walked the cobblestone streets of Boston. We heard about the Boston tea party and studied our history from an early age since we lived so close to where it all happened. The revolution was such a part of our culture they even named our football team the New England Patriots.

Driving around New England it is interesting to see the license plates of various cars. The Connecticut plate has "Constitution state" on it. Massachusetts has "Spirit of America." I like New Hampshire the best: "Live Free or Die." Each of these reflects the essence of America and pride in these states' Colonial heritage.

The Colonial people of that area simply would not tolerate taxation without representation or any other kind of unjust oppression. They craved freedom for themselves and for future generations and were willing to fight for it. I remember learning about the patriot Nathan Hale, who grew up in Connecticut and was captured as a spy for the revolutionaries. He was hanged by the British at the all-too young age of twenty-one years old. Just before he was hanged he was quoted as saying, ("I only regret that I have but one life to give for my country.") I have used this quote when I talk about priesthood: I only regret that I have one life to give for the Lord.

The words of Nathan Hale and Patrick Henry "Give me liberty or give me death!" are etched on my soul. There is such definitive passion in their proclamations. Both these men were totally committed and "all in" with their lives. This is *Give me liberty or give me death!* exactly the way we must be when facing the areas that enslave us. In order to achieve freedom we must have a *holy audacity* and even a *violent* determination. The violence I refer to doesn't mean hurting someone; in this instance, "violence" means an intense energy that urges one to do whatever it takes. In other words, we must have sheer determination and ferocity. This violence is a resolute forcefulness that will not look back.

Jesus spoke of this quality in this enigmatic saying: "The Kingdom of Heaven has suffered violence and the violent take it by force." (Mt. 11:12)

Jesus didn't mean that those who harm others physically will enter God's kingdom. In fact, all his teachings proclaim just the opposite. Jesus preached turning the other cheek and forgiveness. What then, did he mean?

In order to enter God's kingdom you must have a single-hearted forceful energy. You must be determined, unyielding, stubborn, and even violent. You have to fight the good fight of faith, run the race, and not give up. You must turn away from sin, temptation, and stay faithful. These things require energy, endurance, and perseverance. Those who are mediocre and wishy-washy do not possess these qualities. Similarly, in order to struggle free from addictions, bad habits, and behaviors that enslave you, you must have an unbending, even violent mentality. You must be "all in," surrendered and willing to fight.

I am not saying that everything depends on our efforts. On the contrary, we cannot do a thing without the grace of Jesus setting us free. But it is God's grace that brings about this indefatigability and tenacity that will not take no for an answer. "Give me liberty or give me death!" is the violent attitude we must have when facing any substance, person, or behavior that threatens to keep us captive.

Because we live in a democratic society with freedom as our foundation, our country has a tremendous immigration problem. Those who live in oppressive societies with unjust governments are doing everything they can to get into the United States. Many are risking their lives, swarming into overcrowded boats. Others make the dangerous passage through Mexico, where marauders are on the lookout to rob and harm them. Legislators and popular opinion are divided regarding what to do about those who seek to come into our country, as well as those who are already here illegally.

For those who emigrate into the U.S. legally, one of the first things they see if they enter through New York is a large green statue given to us by France. Of course, I am talking about the Statue of Liberty. She graces the New York harbor and holds aloft the torch of freedom for all to see. When I flew into New York recently, the plane banked right over the harbor and I could clearly see this inspiring symbol of freedom. Moments later, I saw the tallest building in the western hemisphere. One World Trade Center, dubbed "The Freedom Tower," was built in lower Manhattan, right over the site of the destroyed World Trade Centers. The spire on top of the building brought the height to exactly 1,776 feet. This symbolic number was, of course, the year the Magna Carter of freedom, the Declaration of Independence, was signed.

I have also visited Philadelphia in my travels. I managed to see another icon of our country's freedom: the Liberty Bell. This bell rang in the tower of the Pennsylvania state house, which we now call Independence Hall. The ringing of this bell called legislators to meetings. In the 1830's the bell gained its significance to liberty and became the rallying cry of the abolitionists trying to end slavery. There is an inscription on the bell taken from Leviticus 25:10: "Proclaim liberty throughout all the land unto all the inhabitants thereof." This verse refers to the Jubilee year in the Bible. Every fifty years property was returned and slaves set free. When Jesus proclaimed his inaugural message in Nazareth, which I referred to earlier, it was a Jubilee proclamation saying his purpose was a ministry of initiating a new time of freedom.

The Liberty Bell developed a crack in the 1840's after ninety years of hard ringing. The wide crack is actually a repair job of a thinner crack. The failed job was abandoned. No one alive today has ever heard the bell ring. Reflecting upon the bell, I believe the crack is symbolic of the abuse of freedom we have. We live in a democratic nation where majority rules. We have been given rights and freedoms from our creator, but we haven't always taken responsibility for the liberties we enjoy. At times we have gone against the will of the One who gave us freedom in the first place. Our abuse of freedom started in Eden and continues exponentially today.

If you read history, it is clear that our founding ancestors meant for our country to be founded on Biblical principles, with God as our center. God is referred to twice in the very first paragraph of the Declaration of Independence. Then we read, "We hold these truths to be self-evident, that all men are created equal, that they are endowed by their creator with certain unalienable rights, that among these are life, liberty and the pursuit of happiness." We read of their understanding of God as our creator and the source of our rights and freedom.

Yet, today there is an abuse of our freedom that goes completely against what our founding ancestors had in mind. We hear about monuments of the Ten Commandments having been taken out of courthouses and schools. Public prayer has been replaced by a moment of silence. Same sex marriages have been legalized. Marijuana is now legal in some states. The problems flowing from this are mounting. The proliferation of school and other shootings is a result of the ease of purchasing firearms. Without a doubt, though, the greatest aberration of freedom is the legalization of abortion in the U.S. This law was signed into effect in 1973. Some have estimated there have been over 57 million abortions in the U.S. since that law was approved. Innocent babies in

A conceived fetus is a child, not a choice.

their mother's wombs have rights, too. A conceived fetus is a child, not a choice.

We must have some sort of compass, some foundation that underlies our freedom or else popular vote will take us places we shouldn't—and do not want—to go. What will be the end of our unbridled democratic freedom? Our nation is in jeopardy.

Please take a moment now and pray for our nation and its legislators. May God have mercy on our nation and bring us to change the unenlightened laws we legislate. In some ways, we are all responsible for this.

Freedom was abused in the Garden of Eden through disobedience. It continues in our own lives when we sin. Freedom's abuse occurs on national levels when we go against our Creator and his will for our lives. With wisdom and understanding we must grasp the intention and context of our founding fathers and use this as a guide when interpreting our rights. Taking our freedom literally and out of context leads to aberrations. Thus, the symbol of our freedom is cracked!

The Bible is full of references to freedom. I have already noted some of Paul's reflections and a couple of Jesus' statements. Perhaps the greatest story illustrating freedom in the Old Testament Scriptures is that of the Exodus. The Hebrews had come to Egypt in the days of Joseph to find food. In time Pharaohs who did not know Joseph began to oppress and force the Hebrew people into harsh work. Their cries reached the ears of God and he raised up Moses as a leader to guide them out of Egypt. The Pharaoh at the time was prideful and obstinate and not willing to let the people go. He forced them into even harder and harsher slavery. Finally, God acted. God performed many signs and wonders and used Moses to lead the people out of Egypt. God's will has been and always will be, "Let my people go!"

The signs God performed were unprecedented and spectacular. God formed a people of his own in the desert and protected them as he led them to the Promised Land. This spectacular exodus became embedded in the Jewish psyche. Remembrance of God's power and desire to free people is celebrated continuously. Feasts and rituals such as Passover and Booths have been celebrated perpetually. The memory of God's liberating deeds brought his powerful grace into the present. This dynamic remembering (anamnesis) would be the foundation for our present-day Mass. At Mass we celebrate the new exodus from slavery to sin and death. Our dynamic remembering of Jesus' passion brings the efficacy of his sacrifice right into the present moment.

Let my people go.

False Freedom

While we are familiar with the concept of freedom, we must be careful not to be misled by what *appears* to be freedom. True freedom isn't liberty from all constraints and restrictions, but well-being in the midst of them. Freedom isn't enjoying the comfortable feelings addictions can bring, but living with self-control and self-restraint.

An example of what I mean is Jesus' statement, "Take my yoke upon you and learn from me…you will find rest for your souls. For my yoke is easy and my burden light." (Mt. 11:29-30) Oxen were connected together by a wooden harness. This wood—or yoke—bound them together as they worked. The rabbis used to speak about the "yoke" of the law. Jesus' commandments are even more radical than the demands of the law. Yet, because of grace, there is an ease, a "rest" about our ability to fulfill his demands.

I remember when I was ten years old I questioned God and the Bible. I curiously read some of the commands in the Bible. I closed the book and looked at the Bible and thought, "Even if God is true, there is no way I could keep all the commands in this book. They are simply too demanding." I felt overwhelmed by the multitude of laws and rules in the Scriptures. I was right. I would never be able to keep them all. But I've found something refreshing.

In Jesus, there is a new ability to be obedient. We have been given a new heart. While I am not perfect, I have a heart for God. Freedom doesn't mean independence from rules and boundaries. Rather, Christian freedom is living under the Lord's yoke with new ease and comfort. The Christian religion shouldn't be a burden (Jesus was talking about the overwhelming demands of the Jewish law when he spoke of burdens) but should lead to inner joy and well-being. Jesus' burden is easy and light. It is possible to follow him without being scrupulous and feeling guilty all the time.

I've heard it said that true freedom is being comfortable within your harness. Some wrongly think that freedom means being without a harness.

Growing up, my best friend's parents divorced. After being married for twenty years and raising four children, my friend's father decided to divorce his wife, leave his job and family, and move away. He found a girlfriend who moved in with him and he lived a completely alternative life. He thought he would find freedom by living this "second childhood," yet, what he found wasn't freedom, but an oppressive yoke. He ended up divorcing his wife, lost contact with his children and didn't find the supposed happiness he thought he would find.

I remember *Thelma and Louise,* a movie that was released in 1991. The movie was about two women, one married and the other dating, who were not happy with their relationships and lives and decided to make a break from the mundane. Their adventure and new-found freedom led to problems and sexual advances from men on many fronts. Because they fought back they ended up in deep trouble with the law. Rather than lose their freedom, they ended up committing suicide by driving their car over a cliff.

Many are seduced by the allure of the supposed freedom adultery brings. Perhaps your spouse doesn't complement you like he used to. You were physically intimate when you were first married, but now the fire has flickered. Suddenly, although you weren't looking for it, there is someone in your life who is paying attention to you and has an interest in you. The excitement brings a seemingly new-found freedom from the blasé of your present lifestyle. Don't let your feelings deceive you. *Every* adulterous relationship will turn out in disaster. Even if you aren't found out, you will be devastated and your relationship with God will suffer. We all remember the movie *Fatal Attraction* that came out in 1987. That movie, starring Michael Douglas and Glen Close, showed the disastrous consequences the so-called freedom of adultery can bring. I've heard it said the fear that movie instilled saved many marriages.

Growing up in our culture, we were given many ideas about freedom that simply weren't true. I remember watching *Happy Days* on television. We all remember the The Fonz, played by Henry Winkler, who, like James Dean, was just too cool for school. While he did have a job as a mechanic, his so-called freedom from studies brought him little. His Don Juan relationships with a variety of women led to an uncommitted lifestyle and he found himself chasing after the wind. He was popular, but ended up with nothing to show for his life. Movies such as the *Harrad Experiment* as well as *Bob & Carol & Ted & Alice* promoted sex and free love, but led to more of the same: ruined marriages and broken lives.

One of the iconic moments that captured the ethos of false freedom was the three-day Woodstock festival. This music festival was held in Bethel, New York, on a dairy farm in August of 1969. It was a time where 400,000 people gathered and lauded the expressions of drugs, sex, and rock and roll. It was a rainy festival. Scenes were shown of drugged people, some naked, slip-sliding away in the mud.

The hippie movement was in full swing at that time, a part of the 1960's counter-culture. They rejected established institutions and middle class values. They embraced sexual liberation and their slogan was, "If it feels good, do it." They grew their hair long, wore earrings and tattoos along with brightly colored clothing. Besides the "flower power" motto, they allowed feelings to be their higher power. Along with the surfers on the west coast who thought ecstasy came from waves, they thought freedom was "doing your own thing."

While such lifestyles did lead to momentary, yet fleeting, pleasures, the end results were not so pleasurable. Free sex led to unwanted pregnancies and sexually transmitted diseases as well as uncommitted relationships that led to hurtful break-ups. Free lifestyles led to poverty and a life devoid of any significance. Liberation from responsibility led to selfish lives that accomplished little. The freedom to experiment with drugs and alcohol led to sicknesses, addiction, and deep despair. Our culture continues to embrace the allure of false freedom. We can emulate others' tragedies and failures, or we can learn from their mistakes.

Work and Freedom

The Nazi regime took another approach. They took the slogan from the title of a novel by Lorenz Diefenbach, *Work Makes You Free,* and publicized it. They had this slogan confront all who entered their concentration camps. Camps such as Auschwitz and Dachau had the statement on the front gates for all to see. After the war, these signs were stolen from both camps, but the one from Auschwitz was later found and placed in a museum.

If following your pleasures doesn't make you free, can arduous work accomplish this feat? The late Holy Father John Paul II promulgated an encyclical *On Human Work* in September of 1981. In this document the Pope talked about the dignity brought to

> *God dignifies our work by being present as we labor.*

humans when they work and how we can transform our society through work. Remember, Jesus called Peter and the other fishermen while they were working. God dignifies our work by being present as we labor.

I have found the work I do brings a great sense of satisfaction. When I am creative, produce, and apply myself, I find I am achieving my potential and fulfilling God's will for my life. Work performed, especially to influence others in a positive way, can bring great inner joy. My finest moments are when I am preaching, hearing confessions, counseling, writing, and producing for television. In that sense, yes, work does bring freedom.

However, work did not bring freedom in the manner it was used by the Nazis. They used work to demean and break the spirits of the men and women in the concentration camps. They forced labor on them to demoralize them. There were 12-14 hour days of hard work that had little or no meaning. They were made to move sandbags, dig ditches or tunnels and then fill them in again. All the while, the prisoners were verbally abused and beaten at regular intervals in order to break their morale.

Today, some people escape their problems and distance themselves from important relationships through their work. Whatever form your work takes, it can be fulfilling and dignifying, but it can also become addictive. While our labors can be liberating, they can also enslave a person. One of the ways to avoid this is to work in moderation and not let it be all-consuming. Work is what you do, not who you are.

It isn't following your desires, lusts, and feelings that leads to freedom. In fact, our feelings are suspect and can easily lead us astray. Think of the saying, "If everyone jumped off the cliff (like Thelma and Louise), would you?" I say, "If everyone is doing it, be careful. It's probably the wrong thing." Remember, feelings are fickle and often deceptive. Many people are led into captivity precisely because they follow their feelings.

While we all want comfortable feelings, true freedom doesn't come from shirking responsibilities and running from issues, but by embracing them. You are truly free when you live within the boundaries of your vocation and the lifestyle you committed yourself to. Don't confuse freedom with lack of responsibility. Being faithful and responsible brings great dignity.

Liberty means being faithful even when you don't feel like it. It means doing the right thing even when it doesn't feel good. It means staying committed even when other options seem more enticing. God longs for our faithfulness. If you embrace

> *Fulfillment lies in being responsible within your vocation.*

the upright vocation and lifestyle God has called you to, you will find deep inner well-being and rest and live a life of ultimate significance. The false freedom of non-commitment is a deep deception. Fulfillment lies in being responsible within your vocation.

Freedom Isn't Free

There is a price to be paid for freedom. We treasure our freedom, but sometimes we forget the cost. Some time ago I visited Washington D.C., and as I walked among the historical sites I came upon a long wall with thousands of names etched upon it. It was the Vietnam Veterans Memorial wall, honoring those who lost their lives in the Vietnam war. The black granite wall contains the names of the over 58,000 men and women who died in service to our country. Over 1,000 of the names are people missing in action.

It is hard to describe the feeling I had standing beside that wall. That memorial is a reflective, quiet, prayerful place. The wall is long and sometimes high, etched with name after name after name. Each carving represents a family, a life, a history. Each person had gifts, goals and dreams. Most of them died all too young. Had not their service taken their life, they would be alive now, enjoying families and jobs and living full lives. Each of them died with courage, fighting for what we now enjoy: freedom.

Near Washington D.C., across the Potomac River, I visited Arlington National Cemetery. Over four hundred thousand men and women from every war we have ever fought are buried there. Crosses and headstones in striking symmetry grace the grassy fields. Row upon row of headstones dot the landscape. This cemetery is yet another sobering, prayerful place that speaks volumes about the cost of freedom. Innumerable brave men and women have given and continue to give their lives so we can live the quality of life we so dearly prize and treasure.

Countless others are wounded warriors. These are the soldiers who have lost limbs or been wounded in a variety of other ways. Some have post-traumatic stress syndrome and are now troubled mentally and emotionally. I was about to board an airplane once, and as we all gathered by the gate the airline official announced, "Any uniformed military person in active duty is free to board the plane first." Two men in the army passed by everyone and proceeded to board the plane. As we watched them pass, the whole group of us burst into applause. They humbly proceeded. I've heard some stories of those in first class who offer their seats to our military personnel. Our fighting men and women live lives of great sacrifice in order to protect and preserve our freedom.

Freedom isn't free. Men and women throughout our history have died and have been wounded so that we may live in freedom. The price of freedom is sacrifice. The cost of freedom is blood.

Similarly, in order for us to be set free from slavery, sin, and death, the Son of God himself suffered and died on a cross. Jesus' passion was the supreme sacrifice. It involved torture, blood, and death. But his sacrifice had ultimate meaning. As he taught, "The Son of Man did not come to be served, but to serve and to give his life as a ransom for many." (Mk. 10:45) Jesus was explaining the meaning of his passion. His crucifixion wasn't some isolated, meaningless event. His self-giving was the ultimate act of service. His death ransoms us from sin, slavery, and death.

A ransom is the price paid to free a prisoner or slave from captivity. Usually, a paid ransom takes the form of money or goods of some sort. We've all heard about Patty Hearst, the daughter of William Randolph Hearst, who was captured by the Symbionese Liberation Army and held for ransom. Millions were paid to get her back. John Paul Getty III was captured by Italian gangsters and held captive. Only after his ear was cut off and mailed to the Italian press was the million-dollar ransom paid to free him.

For our freedom, no amount of money, gold, or goods would suffice. In order to liberate us from our ultimate captor, death, a debt had to be paid. The Old Testament sacrificial system foreshadowed this. Lambs and goats were sacrificed on Passover. Blood was always seen as the purifying element in the Bible because life was thought to be in the blood. On the Day of Atonement, the high priest sprinkled the blood of a goat or bull on the mercy seat to gain forgiveness for the sins of the people.

But when Christ appeared as a high priest of things to come...he entered once and for all into the Holy Place, taking not the blood of goats and calves but his own blood, thus securing an eternal redemption. (Heb. 9:11-12)

Jesus paid a debt he did not owe and we owe a debt we cannot pay.

At the cross, the required blood has been shed. The sacrifice has been offered. A death has occurred. Because of this complete offering of the true unblemished lamb, a new covenant of forgiveness and salvation was established. Our guilt and shame have been healed and we are now right with God, and it is our faith and trust in Jesus' sacrifice on our behalf that justifies us. We have been redeemed. We are ransomed. We are now free. If the Son sets you free, you are free indeed!

I read about an experiment regarding the intelligence of sea animals that was conducted in a southern California aquarium. A barracuda and Spanish mackerel were placed in the same tank. The barracuda is the arch enemy of the Spanish mackerel and uses it as a food source. The scientists

Jesus paid a debt he did not owe and we owe a debt we cannot pay.

placed a clear Plexiglas barrier between the two. As soon as the barracuda saw the other fish he went to attack it and hit his nose on the barrier. He tried again and again with the same result. After repeated attempts he finally gave up. In time the scientists carefully removed the barrier. Even though the barracuda was free to attack and eat the Spanish mackerel, he stayed where he was. He didn't even try because of past conditioning.

Similarly, even though we have been set free by Jesus' passion, we can remain enslaved because of our past conditioning and repeated failures. When Jesus died, the veil in the temple was torn, the barrier removed, and freedom gained. Yet we can be oblivious to the freedom we have and choose to live mired in habitual hurts and conditioned responses. One key step in living free is *knowing* that you are already free! We simply need to walk in the freedom that is ours in Jesus.

Jesus' blood sacrifice initiated this New Covenant:

- Complete forgiveness of any sin past, present or future
- Inner healing from guilt, shame and self-condemnation
- Freedom from ingrained patterned behaviors

A similar truth to the fish experiment happened regarding a lion I heard about. The animal was kept in a small iron cage in a zoo. Day after day it used to stalk back and forth, back and forth. Finally, the zoo obtained a larger cage for the animal so it could have more space. When they put the lion in the larger space he amazed the zookeepers by stalking exactly the same area as when he was in the small cage. Even though he was free to roam a larger distance, he let his past condition him.

When Jesus died, the cage was opened when the veil was torn. We are now free to roam and are no longer trapped by our past. Even though we have hurts and strongholds, we can now move beyond them into the wide open spaces allowed us by the Son of God. Our cage is not only wider, but wide open!

Perhaps you've heard about how trappers catch monkeys in various countries. They place a bunch of firm green bananas in a small cage with bars spaced just wide enough for the monkey to get his arm in there. Once he gets a whiff of those bananas the hungry monkey reaches in and grabs hold of them. But the gap is too small to get the firm bananas out. The monkey clutches at them and tries as hard as he can to get those bananas out. He will not let go of the fruit even though his trappers approach. They say all the trappers have to do is throw a net over the monkey. They open the cage and make him release the bananas and the monkey is caught.

While we have been freed by Christ at the cross, we still hold on to past abuse, hurts and conditioned behaviors, and these memories and behaviors keep us trapped. Our responsibility is to let go. We can't expect someone to pry our fingers open. Rather, grace is present to help us develop new, better behaviors that can replace the old habits that enslave. We let go by developing the courage to face our issues and move through them instead of running from them. Realizing that we are free, we can courageously loosen our grip, hopeful for a fresh new start. You don't have to stay stuck! Christ has set you free.

Here's how to let go:

- Realize you have already been set free
- Live with a "holy audacity" determined to walk in freedom
- Face your issues, don't run from them
- Educate yourself about the issue(s) that enslaves you
- Understand the value of negative reinforcement
- Abandon yourself to God's power to give you success

Remember, you are already free. In 1863, President Lincoln announced the Emancipation Proclamation. This executive order pronounced by the president turned some three million slaves into freed men. Much has been written about the blurred lines of emancipation after that.

Many slaves didn't know about the proclamation and remained slaves. Others, though free, weren't sure where to go or how to make money so they remained slaves because it was sure and safe and all they knew. Imagine living a life of slavery because you don't know you are free or are afraid to forge a better path. This is exactly what happens now in many peoples' lives. They are free, but don't know it. Or, when they find out they are free, they choose to remain slaves because of repetitive habits or because they don't know a better way.

> *Many slaves didn't know about the proclamation and remained slaves.*

It is time to move forward. There is no excuse for staying stuck. Take responsibility for your own freedom, because grace from God is available to help you.

When I lived in Sacramento, California, there was a Passionist retreat center a few miles from downtown. I lived at Christ the King retreat for the first eleven years of my priesthood. In mid-January 1993, I heard about a pro-life rally that was to be held on the capital steps, because Sacramento is the capital of California. It was to take place on January twenty-second, the twentieth anniversary of the legalization of abortion in America. I decided to support the movement by attending.

When I arrived, I saw two groups of people on separate sides of the capital building. The smaller group held signs, coat hangers and made noise. They were the pro-choice people. On the other side of the building was a larger group. They looked very peaceful. Some held babies and others, red roses. They had signs, too. I became a part of this pro-life assembly.

A platform was set up on the top of the steps with a microphone. Soon after I arrived, three women stepped onto the platform and began to speak. I assumed they were the organizers of the event and were going to try to rally the troops. Much to my surprise, they weren't the organizers, but all of them were women who had had abortions! I could hardly believe my ears. The first one stood before the gathered crowd and spoke about the tragedy of her abortion. She spoke of the guilt and shame she has felt for years because of her wrong choice. After her, another woman spoke of her regrets, talking about her misguided choice. I looked around at this pro-life crowd and saw mothers holding their infants. All stood in reverent silence as these women told their stories.

Finally, the third and last speaker got up. She was a woman who confessed to not one, but two abortions. She, too, talked of the paralyzing guilt, shame and self-recrimination she felt. Then she (as had the previous two) got real excited as she shared about Jesus. She said she came to Jesus just as she was: guilty and broken. Jesus mercifully forgave her and brought healing to her life. In her jubilation she jumped up and down as she exclaimed, "I've been set free! I've been set free!" We all applauded her. I was in tears. I've been to many religious services and these testimonies of these three women on the steps of the secular capital building were as reverent and holy as any church service I've ever attended.

Some time ago, I preached a mission in the New Orleans area. Two years later I received a letter from a woman who attended the mission. Here is an excerpt:

I received a miracle at your mission! I had been living with the guilt of abortion for many, many years. It was a constant noose I felt around my neck that would never go away. Although I had worked on my guilt, I still could not forgive myself. It was at your mission that I finally found peace. At one of your services I was consumed with the normal recurring thoughts about my sin, my guilt and my inability to forgive myself. Suddenly I felt a hand on my shoulder and heard a voice, "Enough, already! I forgave you long ago. It is now time for you to move on and forgive yourself." The feeling was so intense that I've never been the same since.

> *I forgave you long ago. It is now time for you to move on and forgive yourself.*

I am so happy for that woman. She experienced firsthand what Jesus came to bring us: freedom from a sinful past. In her case, it was freedom from self-condemnation. As you read this I pray you will sense Jesus saying to you, "Enough already!"

I hear this from so many people: "Father, I know God forgives me, but I just can't forgive myself." I understand that statement. With sin comes guilt and self-recrimination. Because we aren't perfect we reject ourselves and beat ourselves up. We ask, "Am I really that kind of person?" As long as you focus on who you used to be, and the sins you committed, you won't be able to forgive yourself. Rather, you must focus on Jesus' death on the cross and his love for you. In addition to the realization of what Christ did for you, you will receive revelation of his love for you, like this woman did. It may not be as dramatic, but healing nonetheless. One of the worst slaveries is that of chronic guilt and inner condemnation. Beating yourself up relentlessly won't save you. Jesus saves you.

At our retreat center in Houston we have an outdoor reflective place of prayer. The Stations of the Cross wind their way through the garden. I often walk the stations and I am always drawn to the first station where Jesus is condemned. When I meditate on that station I see Jesus standing before Pilate in a dignified posture. Pilate condemns him even though Jesus was innocent. In prayer, I reflect on the truth that Jesus bore *my* condemnation at that moment. No amount of beating myself up and self-recrimination will suffice. I lay my burdens down and allow Jesus to take them from me, for, as the Bible says, "There is now therefore no condemnation for those who are in Christ Jesus." (Ro. 8:1)

We Passionists are called to help others meditate on the Passion of Jesus and derive meaning from his sufferings. One of the greatest purposes of the passion was that Jesus bore our guilt, shame and condemnation. (1 Pet. 2:24)

A major step in the process of letting go is grace. We need power, revelation, help, and God's touch in order to experience freedom. This grace may or may not be accompanied by feelings. Believe in God's free gift.

Don't pray to be set free. Pray to walk in the freedom that is already yours!

Negative Reinforcement

A valuable truth in the process of letting go is something called negative reinforcement. B.F. Skinner was a psychologist who observed human behavior. He pioneered some ground-breaking work in the area of behavior and reinforcement. He noticed that when people received pleasure or reward from their repeated behavior they continued in these actions. As a result, actions were reinforced by pleasurable effects. These good sensations led to ingrained patterned behaviors. As complex as we are as humans, our behaviors are often driven simply by pleasure/reward and the avoidance of pain/punishment. One way to break the habitual behaviors was not only to remove the pleasure but to introduce pain and associate it with the particular pleasurable behavior.

When it comes to an addictive behavior there is always some sort of pleasurable outcome. It could be the high of alcohol, sex, or gambling. Perhaps it is feeling in control or invincible. The pleasure may be escaping pain and feeling free. You may feel a wonderful thrill or tremendous excitement as you participate in the behavior. The more you feel the pleasure, the more ingrained the behavior becomes. However, since humans become tolerant very quickly, you will need an escalating amount of the substance or behavior in order to achieve the same high.

Pain and the perception of punishment associated with a particular behavior have the opposite effect. Negative feelings cause you to want to avoid the behavior. We used to rub our dog's nose in his messes. That stopped his habit of going indoors. Even ingrained habits and addictions can be changed when associated with negative feelings. Long-term illicit relationships such as adulterous liaisons can be broken when the pain of being in the relationship becomes greater than the pleasure associated with it.

Having played golf for over forty years, I derive much pleasure from being out-of-doors and playing in park-like settings. Sometimes there are oceans or mountains near the course. The grass is always green and the area mostly quiet. Since I used to play a lot, I got quite good.

My handicap was below a four and I shot in the 70's quite often. When I hit long drives or made birdies the feeling was quite enjoyable. I would play every chance I got because I derived such pleasure out of golf.

But as I got into my 50's my body began to hurt. Because I swung so hard I began to put stress on my right knee and eventually tore the cartilage on my medial side, resulting in a partial knee replacement. In addition, I have some degenerating discs that flare up occasionally when I play, causing great back pain. When I swung hard my shoulder, neck and hip hurt as well. While this pain made me play less, I didn't stop altogether.

What put me over the top was the pain of ineptitude. Because I was preaching, writing and producing for television, I wasn't able to play much. When I did play, I would be faced with shots that in the past were so easy to make. When I tried to hit those simple shots I couldn't achieve any success with any consistency. I chunked chip shots. I struggled controlling my driver. I missed short putts. In the words of the Beatles song, *Yesterday*, I realized when it came to golf I wasn't "half the man I used to be." I can't tell you the frustration and anger I felt. After several rounds I realized that if I couldn't dedicate time and practice to the game I was destined for more futility and frustration. I simply didn't enjoy the game anymore. Frustration and futility, coupled with the pain in my body, led me to let go of golf. I didn't quit golf, I retired from it when the pain became greater than the pleasure.

Along with the negative reinforcement, I was able to stop because I found a new form of recreation. I have developed a new lifestyle of taking care of my body. Now I'm very much into fitness. Rather than hurting my body, I want to live pain-free. I also devote time to writing each day and producing for television. My ministry is also my hobby. I really enjoy it. Staying fit and ministering to people bring me pleasure. Although it is work, this positive reinforcement has replaced the pleasurable feelings I used to get from golf.

When it comes to an addiction or bad habit, in order to become free you must experience negative reinforcement. Hopefully you will also replace the pleasure the addiction brings with a new and better habit.

The negative reinforcement could be the disaster of a bottoming-out experience. This is when a person who is under the influence behaves in a way that is out of character for them. It could be an accident, a fight, or a black-out experience. Perhaps it is when friends or family confront you with your behavior. The shame and embarrassment of this intervention can be negative reinforcement enough to cause a change.

I visited the family of a friend once. His mother was overweight and was struggling to lose weight. I noticed on her refrigerator door there was taped a picture of a very heavy set woman bending over and you could see the rolls of fat on her legs and behind. Let's just say this gave "bottoming out" a whole new meaning. By putting this picture on her refrigerator this woman was purposely participating in negative reinforcement. The fat woman on the photo was meant to be a deterrent to her overeating. Each time she went to the fridge to get a snack, she was confronted with a painful reminder.

Perhaps one of the greatest examples of sobering pain a person has to face is despair. Despair is the feeling of misery, desolation and despondency one can feel for having failed themselves once again. It is a feeling of guilt and a forlorn attitude of hopelessness. It is the self-recrimination of having let yourself down yet again. This feeling of emptiness is like an emotional and psychological hangover. Once you feel its devastating effects you want to avoid it at all costs. When the scales of negative reinforcement tip in pain's favor, pleasure has to bend. The many facets of negative reinforcement are key triggers for you to let go.

Accountability

I often advise people to go to a group or get a counselor because I realize the value of the counsel and support they will give. But there is another reason I want people to avail themselves to the help of the community. Most feel shame and embarrassment when they admit to a group they have an unmanageable behavior. Seeing a counselor costs money, takes time and it is a hassle to go to them. It is painful exploring issues and delving into your past. Some may need to attend a treatment program lasting a month or longer. At some point in the process you will have an inner dialogue and say to yourself, "Is this pain worth the pleasure of my addiction/habit?" When you are rigorously honest with yourself, your negative reinforcement will outweigh the pleasure of your unwanted behaviors and you will let go of destructive behavior.

Is this pain worth the pleasure of my addiction/habit?

The pain even becomes an accountability factor. When tempted with the illicit behavior, the pain you have suffered will help keep you in line.

Most who submit themselves to a twelve-step program have a sponsor. A sponsor is a person who has wisdom and is willing to walk with you in your journey of recovery. The role of a sponsor is to listen and encourage. The fifth step of the program is confession. You tell your sponsor everything you've done wrong in life. You are only as sick as your secrets. Additionally, a sponsor is also someone you can be accountable to. When you are tempted to fall, you can call your sponsor and talk about it. A paid counselor or group can also have the same function. We can be like little children who need boundaries. A sponsor, group, community, or counselor can be just what we need. You must be responsible and answerable to someone about your behavior. It is dangerous to be only answerable to yourself. When you are struggling with unwanted behaviors, being accountable to someone can be a life saver.

Supernatural Freedom

You are a temple of the Most High. God's Spirit lives in you. Paul wrote, "Where the Spirit of the Lord is, there is freedom." (2 Cor. 3:17) One of the great ministries of God's Spirit in us is to empower us to know and walk in freedom. In his Apostolic Exhortation, *The Joy of the Gospel,* Pope Francis writes,

> There is no greater freedom than that of allowing ourselves to be guided by the Holy Spirit, renouncing the attempt to plan and control everything to the last detail, and instead letting him enlighten, guide and direct us, leading us wherever he wills. The Holy Spirit knows well what is needed in every time and place.
> *(Evangelii Gaudium #280)*

The Spirit of God works within the depths of our conscience to bring healing and new, positive thoughts. I read that a well-known psychiatrist in France commented that humans are comprised of a whole new dimension. We know of our conscious and unconscious makeup. But he introduced the *superconscious*. Because of God, we have an elevated part of ourselves that can lead to great freedom. By getting in touch with our superconscious, we realize we don't have to be consumed by negativity. We can face our fears. We don't have to stay stuck in anger; rather, we can form new habits. We don't have to be overcome by an addiction.

In one of my other books I wrote about my pet spider, Spi. I was standing by my windowsill and I saw a little spider in its web. I was going to kill it and clean the web off but I thought, "It is just a little spider. He isn't hurting anyone." So not only did I not kill him, I adopted him and named him "Spi" the spider. I say hello to him each morning. Sometimes I tweak his web with my finger and he runs around. I splash water on there for him to drink. I enjoy our encounters.

If you have ever gotten your hair caught in a spider's web you know they are sticky. We've all seen flies and other insects who are trapped in a web. Have you ever wondered why the spider doesn't get stuck in his own adhesive web? It is because spiders secrete a special oil that enables them to glide easily on the web itself without getting stuck. Similarly, you are anointed with the oil of the Holy Spirit. You were not meant to stay stuck in life, but to glide easily through it.

One of the great mantras in charismatic circles is "The anointing breaks the yoke." This saying comes from the *King James Bible* translation of Isaiah 10:27. You are anointed by the Holy Spirit. Whatever yoke or burden you bear is broken by God's Spirit. We simply need to agree with this work of the Spirit and allow ourselves to be led by God. It is those who

> *The anointing breaks the yoke.*

are led by God who are his true children. God whispers freedom in the depths of the Spirit.

Responsibility

God will certainly do his part in us, but we must do our part, too. One of the fallacies about freedom is that we will feel free or experience a burst of power to make us free. While that may occur, for the most part, freedom is a process of taking responsibility for our behavior and thoughts (a process is an ongoing activity of progress and moving forward).

Most of you know I write often about the twelve-step program. While I am not a member of any twelve-step program, countless people come to our retreat center who are. I have ministered to some by participating in retreats and by hearing them review their fifth step. As I said before, the fifth step is like a confession wherein a person reveals their past failures and darkest secrets.

I've learned so much about personal change and progressing forward from the various twelve-step programs and from those in recovery. The program is based on good, solid Christian principles and is applicable to anyone struggling with an addiction, bad habit, or sin.

One major truth I've learned is that the journey to freedom (recovery) is a process. You never really arrive; you are always on the way. Even if you aren't drinking or gambling or shopping, you are still in process. You may be sober but you will still need to get to the root of the issue(s) that caused the addiction in the first place. Perhaps the most well-known phrase in the program is "one day at a time." This wonderful attitude means you realize your life is in process and you work on yourself each day, one day at a time. You don't get overwhelmed by seeing how much you have to do when you take things one day at a time. You are able to stay sober when you concentrate only on the day at hand, not on tomorrow. This is a truth Jesus taught when he said, "Don't be anxious about tomorrow. Let each day's trouble be sufficient for each day." (Mt. 6:34)

I think most people envision freedom as an all or nothing situation. Either you are free or you aren't. Actually, there are various degrees of freedom. We advance along a spectrum. Movement along a spectrum is now the present-day thinking in many twelve-step circles. In the past it was thought you are either addicted or not. Now it seems clear that there is a whole range regarding addictions, from slightly/mildly-addicted to extremely addicted. When you are out of kilter regarding a substance or behavior, you have to determine where you are along the spectrum.

The twelve-step program tries to deal with unwanted behaviors first and then delves into the root of these behaviors. Major advancement and progression in unwanted behaviors can occur, but inner issues still need to be dealt with. There is the concept of a "dry drunk." This is a person who has stopped his or her drinking, but they aren't dealing with the issues that led to their drinking in the first place. Thus, they haven't come to the fullness of freedom they can achieve.

There are many causes or roots to addictions of every sort. Certainly, escape from any type of pain is a major factor. Simply wanting to savor pleasure and the high is another factor. Psychologically, one of the major roots may be shame. Shame, of course, was the first effect of original sin. Adam and Eve were free from any self-consciousness in the garden, but when sin was introduced a feeling of disconnect from God, self and others was immediately felt. They became self-aware and felt naked. One of the effects of shame is feeling embarrassed about yourself. You don't feel good enough and feel less than others. You aren't ashamed about what you do, but with who you are. You are ashamed of and reject yourself interiorly. The pain of shame causes some people to seek comfort in some type of activity that becomes an addiction. For a brief moment you can escape the pain, but once the high wears off, the despair and regret come crashing in even more heavily. Addictions are a vicious cycle of pain, escape and even more pain.

Freedom isn't so much God parting the Red Sea and drowning the Egyptians as God working in us and with us to help us face our issues and move forward. Freedom is less a deliverance and more a process. Freedom isn't free. There is a price to be paid and the cost is personal responsibility.

> *Freedom is less a deliverance and more a process.*

Here are some important facts, that when faced, lead to greater degrees of freedom behaviorally and internally.

You can experience personal freedom when:

- You are rigorously honest with yourself
- You admit your unwanted behaviors and moral failures
- You surrender to God, who has freeing power
- You continue in the educative and learning process

On just about every mission I preach I hear many confessions. I preach a lot about the value of confession and its healing power. James, in his letter tells us, "Confess your sins to one another that you may be healed." (Jas. 5:16) Along with the cathartic value, confession is a sacrament that mediates grace. Through it, you can experience the resurrection power of God.

In the confessional, some will come to me and admit they have an addiction or some other moral failure. They have examined their conscience, reviewed their life, and been rigorously honest. They have admitted they have a problem(s) and are willing to reveal their secrets. In the confessional, they are publicly surrendering to God and are humble enough to accept counsel from a priest. They receive absolution. While this is wonderful and crucial, most think that is all that needs to be done.

I hesitate to let a penitent with addictive tendencies go without instructing them further. Coming to confession can be healing and powerful, but it is only a first step. I always tell people, "Now you need to follow-up on what you have done here or you risk falling right back into the same behaviors you just confessed."

People who are out of control need more than forgiveness. They need personal responsibility and accountability. Say, for example, the person admits to overeating and not being able to control their cravings. They may be very contrite and determined to change, but they will need more than forgiveness. They may need to join a recovery group and strive for sobriety through the group. Others who find groups too embarrassing need to seek out an addictions counselor to explore their behavior and inner issues. Most will need a sponsor, spiritual director or trusted friend they can talk to and be accountable to.

Also, those struggling need to educate themselves in the area where they are struggling. Say you wrestle with anger and not forgiving someone who has hurt you. Purchase a book about anger and read about the issue. Determination alone will not get it done. You need the support of the community. You need to educate yourself about your issue and yourself. There are books galore about the multitude of issues people face. Learning about the nature of the disease itself can lead to personal growth. There are helps in the community for any addiction. Simply google any behavior problem with your zip code and you will find places to go.

You might remember the TV mini-series, *Roots,* that aired on television in 1977. It was based on Alex Haley's novel, *Roots: The Saga of an American Family.* The series starred LeVar Burton in the role of Kunta Kinte and explored his roots growing up in Africa and being taken as a slave to America. The series followed the family through the civil war to eventual freedom. Just as racial slavery has roots, so, too, does personal slavery.

The reason I strongly advise those coming to me to confession to follow up by attending a group, seeing a counselor, and reading about their issues is because they need to explore their roots. Unwanted behaviors are one thing, but what causes the acting out is another. The root of the issue must be dealt with. If you pick a dandelion and expect it to disappear, you will be mistaken. The weed will appear again in just a few days. However, if you dig up its roots, I can guarantee you will not see that dandelion in your yard again.

The root of the issue must be dealt with.

When you attend a twelve-step group you learn about yourself by hearing the stories of others who are struggling with similar issues. You gain the support of others through their stories and encouragement. Most people seek out a sponsor who will work closely with them. If you choose to spend time with a counselor you can learn about the nature of habitual unwanted behaviors. You can also explore your own psychological makeup and determine what is causing your unwanted behaviors. Perhaps you struggle with low self-esteem. You may have a controlling nature. You may be overworked and under a lot of stress. You may simply be perpetuating the dysfunctional behaviors of significant others. Whatever the cause, the root of the issue needs to be understood and dealt with.

Talking with a counselor is a form of accountability. Left to ourselves, we can be like unsupervised children in need of parental authority. A group or counselor makes us accountable. This is one of the purposes of having a sponsor. This person stays in close contact with you, especially in the beginning. You are able to call them 24/7 when you are struggling with emotions or unwanted behaviors. They help you to be strong and fight the good fight. Having the support of others and developing boundaries for accountability is necessary in order to come to sobriety. You can also use these helps even if your behaviors are not addictive. This is why going to confession frequently helps people overcome habitual sins and nagging bad habits.

As I was writing this chapter, something wonderful happened. President Obama ordered restoration of full diplomatic relations with Cuba. There is now a loosening of travel restrictions and our past economic sanctions toward Cuba. Our embassy that had been closed for some 50 years has now been reopened. This action was actually facilitated behind the scenes by Pope Francis, who encouraged talks between our President and Raul Castro. Let us hope that our communist neighbor to the south will now begin to taste and adopt the precepts of freedom that we enjoy.

Paving the way for diplomatic relations with Cuba was the release of Alan Gross, a political prisoner. He was arrested while working as a U.S. government contractor and accused of spying for the U.S. He was held in a Cuban prison for over five years. Upon his release, *ABC News* showed video footage of him flying home and being reunited with his family. The jubilation on Alan's face as he was reunited with his family was powerful. For the first time in five years, he was free.

There are definite benefits to freedom! There is personal dignity. There is joy. You have inner peace and self-contentment. You have room to become all you have the potential to be. God created us free and desires our personal freedom.

The prospect of freedom challenges us to reach new heights! The desire for freedom is in our blood, our D.N.A. Freedom is your right and heritage. Don't settle for anything less than your own liberty. While there is an extreme cost to freedom, the price has been paid. The blood has been shed. We have been ransomed and Christ has set us free. Grasp the liberty that is yours. Take responsibility for your own freedom, be audacious and aggressive, and have the daring attitude of Patrick Henry, who, in his impassioned plea before the Continental Congress exclaimed, "Give me liberty or give me death!" You were made to walk in freedom and your personal liberty will bring a whole new self-appreciation and joy. Don't settle for anything less.

4
THE CHALLENGE OF DEATH

I have vowed myself to the Passionist Community. St. Paul of the Cross founded our community in the 1700's. Often he is pictured praying before a crucifix. If you look closely at the crucifix it has a skull and crossbones at the bottom of the cross. This is true of the profession crucifix which I was given as well. Why such a morbid symbol? The skull and crossbones were meant to remind us of our own death. Often, we live as though we are forgetting we will one day die. As we are reminded about our own death we cannot help but become better people. Our own certain death is a solemn wake-up call.

A 78-year-old friend of mine emailed me and said he made the arrangements for his own grave and tombstone so his wife wouldn't have to deal with funeral details when he died. He went to the graveyard and saw his final resting place. He stood and stared at his own tombstone, observing the details, and he saw his name and the date of his birth. The only thing missing was the date of his death. He said seeing his own tombstone was a sobering wake-up call for him.

On Ash Wednesday, Catholics are reminded of our own mortality as we enter the season of Lent. As we are ashed we hear, "Remember, O Man, that you are dust and to dust you shall return." Lent is a sobering season that demands personal change. We turn away from sin and dedicate ourselves to self-discipline and good works of every sort.

You probably don't know what you'll be wearing when you are buried. I do. We religious live simple lives and we don't own anything. We have forfeited all worldly goods by professing our vow of poverty. When I preach or produce television programs I do so donned in my black religious habit. It is a simple garment proclaiming my consecration toward Jesus and my love for his passion. I am very aware that I will be wearing my habit when I am laid out in my casket.

When I studied in Rome, I remember seeing Bernini's guilded bronze statue of a skeleton holding an hourglass in St. Peter's basilica. The statue is called *memento mori*, Latin for "Remember: you, too, will die." The statue is a sobering reminder that our days are numbered and death will be a reality to all of us.

We are not a death-denying Church. We are a death-*defying* Church.

The Psalmist wrote, "Teach us to number our days that we may gain wisdom of heart." (Ps. 90:12) In other words, the Scriptures are telling us to come to grips with the reality of our own death and prepare for it. Wisdom dictates, "Later always comes." Our own deaths challenge us to live well now so that we will be prepared for our own passing. Most live as if they will never die. We know better.

For the past fifteen years, I have spent hours upon hours writing. I gather stories, research theology, and share personal experiences, spending large amounts of time in front of my computer, typing. However, I am not the only one writing a book. We are all writing our own personal book by the way we are living. That is exactly what the Scriptures teach. Revelation records, "I saw the dead, great and small, standing before the throne, and books were opened. And the dead were judged by what was written in the books, by what they had done." (Rev. 20:12)

This passage is telling us that every day we are writing paragraphs of our lives and as time goes on, chapters in our own personal book. Day by day, month by month, year by year, what we do and say is recorded in this book. Like it or not, we are all authors. Each of us has a thick book with our name in gold glittering calligraphy on the cover. Every thought, every deed, every motivation

> *Every day we are writing chapters of our lives.*

is in there. One day your book will be opened before God and its contents revealed. What will it contain? Will the chapters display selfishness, or selflessness? Will there be passion, or passivity? Will you achieve your potential, or be satisfied with mediocrity? Will you impact people for God, or will you stay silent, afraid to speak? Did you love God, or love yourself more? Did you believe in Jesus as your personal savior?

The good news is that your book isn't finished yet. There is still time. You are writing the content of that book now. What is written will be definitive and clear. The finality of our death challenges us to make its pages something we will be proud of. What will your legacy be? When that book is opened, will you be proud or ashamed of what you said, what you did, what is written in there for all to see? We will be judged by what we have written in its indisputable pages.

It isn't so much how the book started as how it finishes that really matters. Our upcoming deaths lay a claim on us to write our books well and reach higher levels of spirituality. Our future death challenges us to be ready.

I enjoy walking in cemeteries. I find them peaceful, quiet places. Seeing the multitudes of people who have gone before me makes me very reflective. Often, we lose touch with the reality of our own impending death. Being confronted by tombstones makes it clear. What has happened to every person who has ever lived will happen to us, too. Each headstone is a story, a life lived. Some have epitaphs. An epitaph is a saying or Biblical quote on a tombstone. If I were to choose one it would be, "I am convinced that not even death can separate us from the love of God that comes to us in Jesus Christ." (Ro. 8:38)

> *Often, we lose touch with the reality of our own impeding death.*

I heard about a humorous epitaph from Key West Florida. It read:

As you are now, so once was I
As I am now so you will be
Prepare for death and follow me!

Underneath, someone humorously wrote:

To follow you I'll not consent
Until I know which way you went!

Hebrews 9:27 tells us, "It is appointed for people to die once and after that comes the judgment." And Benjamin Franklin quipped, "There are two things we can count on: death and taxes." We have all been to funerals, we have all seen cemeteries, and we all know people who have died. My ninety-year old mother passed to the Lord in August 2014. One of our priests was making candles as a part of his ministry and he had a heart attack and suddenly died. We were all shocked, as he was only seventy-two and not sick. The older I get, the more people I know who have passed. Relatives, friends, community members have all gone before us.

Death is everywhere. We hear about death in the news every day. We are well aware that our own death is a certainty, but questions remain. How will we die? Where will it occur? When will it happen? What will it be like? These questions demand that we trust in God. No one knows the day or the hour of their death. No one knows exactly what the future holds, but we can trust in the One who holds the future in his hands. Life and death are in God's hands. (Job 12:10)

The apostle James tries to put us in touch with the passing nature and brevity of our life. He wrote, "You do not know about tomorrow. What is your life? For you are a mist that appears for a little time and then vanishes." (Jas. 4:14) I saw a preacher demonstrate this sobering truth. She stood there with a can of hairspray and pressed the nozzle. A short burst of spray was shot and quickly dispersed. Isn't life like that?

I went on a vacation some time ago. It seemed to be lasting a good long time, but suddenly it was over. That is also the way our lifespan will be.

There is a website: www.worldometers.info that I find fascinating. The site shows in real time the ascending numbers of the world population. At the time of this writing there are 7.3 billion people in the world. What is fascinating is how the site shows the world-wide rate of births and real time rate of deaths. Every second about five people are born. Every second about two people die. There is a constant parade of people coming and going. Both our birth and death are natural, common, ordinary, everyday occurrences. Yet it seems to us as if our death is not natural. We view death as something uncommon and gut-wrenching.

Death and the Bible

The Scriptures have much to teach us about our perspective on death. While natural and inevitable, we read that our death was caused by our own sin. (Gen. 3:3) The wages of sin is death. God is not the author of death; he created us for incorruption, but through the envy of the devil, death entered the world. (Wis. 2:23-24) Paul the apostle writes about death being our enemy, which will one day be destroyed. (1 Cor. 15:26) I want to make this clear: evil and sin caused death, not God. In the Bible, death is seen as the enemy, yet an enemy that has been defeated.

I know of many people, myself included, who struggle with the fear of death. The letter to the Hebrews tells us this is a common phenomenon. In the last chapter I wrote about slavery and freedom. Perhaps the greatest bondage is the constant fear of death. We read in the Scriptures:

> Jesus became human that through death he might destroy him who has the power of death, that is, the devil, and deliver all those who through fear of death were subject to lifelong bondage.
>
> (Heb. 2:14-15)

A place I love to visit is Hearst castle near San Simeon, California. This huge mansion spreads out for miles on the enchanted hills overlooking the Pacific coast highway and the Pacific Ocean. I have toured the opulent, ornate mansion many times. I've seen historical artifacts, many of them religious, gathered from around the world, and walked on the mosaics made of gold that surround the pool. Hearst's mansion gives opulence and extravagance a whole new meaning.

William Randolph Hearst was a newspaper magnate who accumulated vast wealth. He entertained famous guests at his mansion. Even though he was married, Hearst had a long affair and lived with actress Marion Davies at what he called "the ranch." Perhaps, because of a troubled conscience as the result of the affair, he had a standing rule at his ranch. No guest of his could ever mention the word "death" in a conversation. Each night he was afraid to go to sleep because of his fear of death. He eventually did die in 1951 at the age of eighty-eight. His precious ranch was given to the state of California and is now a place for visitors to tour.

Christianity is a religion that doesn't fear death. Paul the Apostle points his finger at death and gets feisty. He shouts, "Death, where is your victory? Death, where is your sting? Thanks be to God who give us the victory in our Lord Jesus Christ!" (1 Cor. 15:55-57) As I've said, ours is not a death-denying church, but a death-*defying* church. We don't skirt around the issue of death, we confront it. In the funeral liturgy we look square in the face of death and proclaim, "Life has *changed*, not ended."

Despite the certainty of victory that is ours, there are still many unknowns. The fear of death has many facets, so questions remain. When will it happen? How will death occur? What will it be like? It is most distressing to those whose consciences aren't right before God and to those who have no faith. Many who haven't lived well suffer from regret and panic as they age.

Along with the fear of death, most are terrified about the dying process itself. There are so many questions such as: As I age, will my health fail? Will I develop Alzheimer's? Will I need to go into assisted living or a nursing home? Will I live too long in poor health? The fear of death and the dying process is a great affliction. But believers in Jesus know that he came to deliver and free us from the sting and bondage of death. However long we live, in whatever health, we are assured God will never forsake us. In Jesus we have tremendous hope.

While death is seen as an enemy in the Bible, we are given great hope. For example, one verse from the Psalms is often proclaimed at funerals. It is Psalm 116:15, which states, "*Precious* in the eyes of the Lord is the death of one of his faithful ones." (italics added) Far from being unnoticed, this verse tells us that God not only notices but cares deeply about our death. My mother used to have a cat named Precious. She loved that cat and was always asking, "Where's Precious?" The cat was dear to her and extremely valuable. She made sure when she died that Precious would be taken care of by my cat-loving sister. We are dear to God. He watches over us and will take care of us when we need it most. Our lives are in God's hands and our inevitable death is known to him.

In 2 Timothy 4:6 Paul reflects upon his own death and writes, "The time of my departure has come." When Moses and Elijah appeared to Jesus on the Mount of Transfiguration they spoke about Jesus' future death as his departure. (Luke 9:31)

I fly on planes quite a bit. The gate where you wait to board the plane is also referred to as the departure lounge. Planes depart from one destination to another. Similarly, the Bible is telling us that when we die we will depart, not cease to exist. We leave for another destination. A believer's destiny is God himself, and then life with him in heaven, our true home. Life has not ended, but changed.

Death is spoken of many times in the Scriptures as "sleep." When Jesus speaks of Lazarus or the young girl who died he refers to them as "sleeping." Paul speaks of those who have died as "asleep." (1 Thess. 4:13,15) We know when a person is asleep that their unconscious faculties are still working. We dream and our bodily functions still work. Eventually we awake. We need sleep to refresh us and renew our tired bodies. Likewise, the sleep of death will not mean life has ceased. We will be with God, more alive than ever.

In Philippians 1:20-24, we read that Paul was wrestling with his imprisonment and struggles with his sufferings. Since he had been caught up to heaven and heard inexpressible things, Paul knew of the glories to come. As he reflected he made a powerful statement: "For me to live is Christ and *to die is gain*." (italics added) We usually talk about death as being a loss, but Paul calls it gain. The reason we gain when we die is because, as Paul put it, "My desire is to depart and be with Christ, for that is far better (than life here)." Death in the Bible is spoken of as a passageway to our ultimate destination. Our purpose is to live with God in heaven forever. That is why we refer to death as a "passing." We are told not to grieve as those who have no hope. (1 Thess. 4:13)

> *For me to live is Christ and to die is gain.*

Grieve Well

As I mentioned before, just before I began this book, the love of my life, my mother, died at the age of ninety, on August 17, 2014. She had a heart valve problem that became critical. We made the family decision to try surgery in order to extend the length and quality of her life, but she suffered a massive stroke during the operation. She lived for eleven days after the surgery. My two sisters and I were by her side as she took her last breath. She was sedated and well taken care of. I anointed her and prayed by her bedside as she went to the Lord.

I was devastated and felt like a dish that had been smashed. The woman who loved me unconditionally and who nurtured me from infancy was now gone. I saw the last breath of the person who saw my first breath. My emotions were all over the place and overwhelming. The Lord granted me sleep during those days of her sickness and death. Were it not for grace, I don't know how I would have slept at all.

Being with my mother when she passed was a blessing and a great help in the grieving process. Seeing her breathe her last brought a sense of finality to me. I was able to tell her I loved her over and over and hold her hand and kiss her. I spoke words of faith into her ear as she was growing weaker. I assured her of Jesus' love for her. As I loved her at her bedside this helped me to grieve. Seeing her take her last breath is a moment I will never forget.

I presided at her funeral a few days after she passed. The celebration was at her church in Florida, where I was known because I had just preached a mission there some months prior. There was a wonderful outpouring of cards, prayers and love. My friends came from as far away as Oregon, Houston, and Louisville. The local community and priests supported me. Even those on my Facebook page helped me to grieve with their prayers and sentiments. I begged God to help me preside and preach well and God answered my prayers; the funeral was simple and celebrated her life and faith in God. Presiding and preaching was my final way to honor her.

Grieving isn't easy. It is an emotional suffering that comes to everyone. I actually helped myself by grieving ahead of time, preparing myself emotionally for my mother's death. I knew it was coming and had many inner conversations with myself about it. When I was on retreat a few months earlier, I woke up one night and wrote her funeral homily. Advance preparation is a way you can help yourself to grieve.

The number-one thing I encountered when Mom died was shock and sadness. I also felt bewildered. Even though I was prepared and knew it was coming, Mom's death was a shock. Her passing was hard to accept and believe. I had never known life without her—she was the woman who loved me unconditionally. She was a constant source of support, and now she was gone. The loss was definite and irreversible. I felt a deep sadness. I was able to function and laugh with people, but when I was alone my emotions overwhelmed me. The feelings came in waves. I had good moments and very difficult moments.

Right after she died, the mornings, just after I woke up, were the hardest. My mind wasn't yet occupied with day-to-day living and distractions. As I lay in bed I thought of negative things such as, "How will I live without her? I'll never see her again. I need her support. I want to talk to her." One of the hardest things was knowing I could never talk to her on the phone again, because I used to call her all the time.

After a few days of concentrating on the negative, I realized I had a choice. I found I could purposely choose to focus on the positive. I decided to think about the realities I also knew were true: She no longer suffers. She is with God. Mom is reunited with my dad. I had the comfort of being with her when she passed, and one day we will be reunited. And one thought that was a great source of comfort to me was, "It was her time." She lived a good, full life and I really believe God *summoned* her home. As I mentioned before, Paul wrote, "We do not grieve like the rest of humanity who have no hope." (1 Thess. 4:13) Paul was saying we don't have to stay stuck in negativity. We have a glorious hope that will help us through the pain of loss.

A friend of mine just lost her mother to death, at the time of this writing. This woman is a great benefactor of my ministry. It was her mother who discovered my television program and she told my friend about me. When her mother passed I called my friend and expressed my sympathy. She was so upbeat and she talked about her mother's faith and the celebration (funeral) to come. I told her, "You sound great, and everyone should see death the way you do. Your mother had a deep faith, and it is wonderful that you see her passing as a time to celebrate and rejoice." Truly, Christians don't grieve like the rest of the world.

When it comes to grieving, time always heals. I am writing this four months after my mother died. The initial shock has worn off and the sadness has lifted. I still experience the pain of her loss, but I have moved on. I've noticed, that especially early on, there were good days and not so good days. Some days the flood of emotions and difficult thoughts will be overwhelming. Other days, you are stronger and able to accept the reality of death. In time, the good days outnumber the hard days. When someone dies, I always tell their family and friends to "grieve well." What I mean is, feel the pain and move forward—don't stay stuck in sadness and negativity; rather, focus on the positive. God is there to help you move into a better place emotionally.

God has helped me every step of the way. I lean on God and rely on God. I don't always feel the help, but sometimes I feel a loving touch by the Holy Spirit. Whether I feel it or not, I know God is there to help me. I invited God into the grieving process. Through Him, I was able to witness my mother's death, preside at her funeral, and let go of the house where I lived for thirty years, as well as move through the pain.

It is God who helps us through the various stages of grief and brings us to acceptance. Elisabeth Kubler Ross wrote a classic book about grief called, *On Death and Dying*. In this important book she listed five main stages of grief:

- Denial: Losing your loved one is simply hard to believe

- Anger: Toward death, toward life and sometimes toward your loved one, yourself, and even God.

- Bargaining: You bargain with God, and even death, about your loved one. You want to know where they are and even talk to them.

- Depression: The negative feelings are overwhelming at times

- Acceptance: You finally agree with what has occurred and try to see the good in it. You become more positive and feelings don't overwhelm you.

It should be noted that these stages aren't necessarily sequential. Even when you are in acceptance, negative feelings and anger may still come. There is a kaleidoscope of feelings that swirl about you. We are all human, but everyone grieves differently. Many have found grief groups and talking things out with others to be extremely helpful. Accept your humanity and the way you grieve.

> *Accept your humanity and the way you grieve.*

God-Incidences

I remember hearing stories about how, when some die, they see angels or report seeing loved ones coming to receive them home. Relatives say they feel a peace in the room that is palpable. I half-way expected something supernatural when I stood by Mom's deathbed, but nothing out of the ordinary happened. There were no visitations from angels or feelings of peace. I think this is the way it is for most people. There is only the reality of your loved one dying.

Others talk about seeing signs after the death. God will give evidence that your loved one is alive and well. The manifestation could be a voice, music, a striking coincidence of some sort, like a bird or rainbow or a prearranged sign that comes true. I've heard a variety of things from several people, and I wondered why I wasn't receiving anything. There were no signs, no verifications, no coincidences. I simply had to trust that Mom was with God and that she was okay.

However, four long months after her death, I spent a few weeks in Mom's house before my sisters sold it. My mother's bed was a place where I connected with her. Several times I would pray the liturgy of the hours by her bed. One time as I was praying I was distracted. Out of the corner of my eye, through the window, I saw two yellow butterflies flitting around and landing on the blossoms on one of the bushes in the yard. My parents loved to garden and that bush is something I had seen both of them work on together. Their whole yard was full of plants, bushes and green grass.

Butterflies flit about and go wherever they want. They are free because they have first suffered. Their struggle and transformation have brought them a whole new liberty. As I looked out the window, I saw not one, but two yellow butterflies encircling and bumping into each other. I interrupted my prayer and stared out the window. As I watched, they would land on the blossoms and spiral upwards in an aerial dance. It was uncanny. I didn't see any butterflies around before or after this incident. I couldn't help but think of both Mom and Dad, and I was comforted. I felt like I was witnessing a moment where God was telling me that not only are my parents alive, but they know a new freedom and enjoy each other more than ever before. I was truly touched. I will never forget the moment of grace that occurred in the context of my prayer by her bed. I think God gives these signs to all of us at some point. Yet, most people aren't aware of these "God-incidences."

At the hospital, when my mother had suffered the stroke after her operation, they put her in palliative care. The focus shifted from helping her get well to comforting her in her last days. I saw one of the nurses paste a purple butterfly to the sliding door window in her I.C.U. room. That butterfly symbolized that death was near. I have an affinity with butterflies. I told the story of the caterpillar and metamorphosis in my first book, *Live Passionately!*

A woman in Michigan heard me tell that story of suffering and change and painted a lovely butterfly for me. I liked it so much I put that artwork on the cover of the book.

Grieving is a season in our lives. I wrote a book called *Seasons of Life*, and in this book I explain that growing up in New England we encountered four well-defined seasons. Each had its own character and lasted a specific amount of time. Ecclesiastes tells us there is a time and season for everything. There is a time to laugh and a time to cry, a time to grieve, and a time to dance. (Eccl. 3:1,4) We learn from each season we experience. But there is always another season on the horizon. Weeping may endure for the night, but joy comes in the morning. (Ps. 30:5) If you are in a grieving season, I pray you will embrace it, let it change you, then move on to the next thing God has for you. Let your grieving mold you, but don't stay stuck in it. God has much more for you in the future.

The death of my father really helped me when dealing with my grief for my mother. My dad died suddenly in his sleep fourteen years ago. My dad was my best friend. I am Cedric Junior, and I bear his name. I had never had anyone close to me die before. Suddenly, I was thrust into the grieving process. I was devastated. Having to preside at his funeral was the hardest thing I have ever done. I grieved intensely the first few years after he passed.

My Dad's death and the aftermath helped me when I had to face my mother's passing. To some degree, I knew what to expect when the Lord took my mother home. I was able to preside at Mom's funeral with much more confidence. The challenge of my dad's death and grieving had changed me.

The truth proclaimed in this book is that when we face challenges of every sort, they change us and make us better. They equip us to be able to face similar, and even harder, challenges in our future. The feelings and emotions you experience when a loved one dies will help you to face the deaths of others, and prepare you for your own eventual passing. Also, your challenges can make you a source of comfort to others when they go through their own grieving.

> *Your challenges can make you a source of comfort to others when they go through their own grieving.*

As a priest, I meet people all the time who have lost others. Because of my experience, I can truly sympathize and feel their pain.

Views on Death

When it comes to death, there are basically three philosophies people can have. These opinions have many nuances, but mostly fall into these categories:

- When you die, you cease to exist. There is no more.
- You will be reincarnated and return as someone else.
- You will go to God and continue to live.

I've met people who subscribe to one or the other of these views. Cultures and religions embrace them in various ways.

Questions regarding the ultimate confront every person who lives. Is there a heaven and hell? What happens when I die? Is there an afterlife? What has happened to my loved ones who have died? Then, of course there is the God question: Is there a God or not?

These questions demand answers. Some think there is no way to find the answers to these questions so they don't try. Thinking like this is fatalism. Jesus taught quite the opposite. He said we should search for God and our questions will be answered. These words of Jesus, from Matthew 7:7, changed my life: "Ask and you shall receive, seek and you will find, knock and the door will be opened."

When I was eighteen years old I was struggling emotionally and spiritually. I had been born and brought up Catholic, but like so many other teens, had fallen away from my faith. I was a freshman in college and was encountering many different ideas and philosophies, meeting many different people who had a wide variety of opinions about life and its meaning. I had just gone through a breakup with a young woman and was devastated inside. In my quest for understanding, I turned to the Bible for answers. When I came upon Matthew 7:7 the words of Jesus touched me. I saw that even though I don't understand now, perhaps God would reveal truth to me if I kept at it. The verse sparked hope, and I prayed for wisdom and understanding. I asked for help. The unknown and my unhappiness were challenging me to find solutions, so I turned to the God of my youth.

When hard questions confront you, you can do one of two things. You can throw your hands up and say, "No one knows the answers to these things. Why even try?" Or, you can pursue truth with hope. I chose to seek wisdom believing we can know the answers to the ultimate questions we face. The answers we crave can be found and are within our grasp if we are dedicated to the search. Our own mortality challenges us to find answers.

In Catholic tradition, the book of Wisdom is an approved book in the Bible. This book lauds the virtue of understanding and those who seek her treasures. I was drawn to this book and with delight I read,

Therefore I prayed and understanding was given to me; I called upon God and the spirit of wisdom came to me. I do not hide her wealth, for wisdom is an unfailing treasure for people; those who get wisdom obtain friendship with God, commended for the gifts that come from instruction.

(Wis. 7:7,13,14)

The most sincere desire to learn is the true beginning of wisdom. We were made for learning and growth in understanding. Little children are always asking questions. When did we stop asking? There are answers to questions if we will but search them out. Not all answers come quickly, nor are they readily apparent. Many hidden answers only come by revelation.

> *The most sincere desire to learn is the true beginning of wisdom.*

Wisdom is not only the virtue of learned experience but of a Spirit who loves us. Wisdom, learning, and understanding are alive. King Solomon prayed for wisdom and was given an understanding heart, and in the book of Proverbs he counsels us to seek understanding like silver and search for it as for hidden treasures. (Pro. 2:4)

After many months of diligent seeking and asking, the spirit of wisdom came to me and revealed to me treasures that would change my life and lead to my becoming a Catholic priest. Often, I'll be sitting in the presider's chair looking out at the congregation of one thousand people and shake my head. How in the world did all this happen? I was never even an altar boy growing up. I was never very religious. What happened was the Spirit of Wisdom revealed some of her precious understanding to me. The ultimate truths I was given completely revolutionized my life. I professed my vows as a Passionist and became a priest. I will never be the same, and I want to share some of what I have been given with you.

I wrote a book called *Death, the Final Surrender*. In this, my best-selling book, I shared about my two near-death experiences right after I turned nineteen. These experiences were beyond words and were the source of a rebirth and change-of-life for me. What happened to me changed the way I think about death and life. Words convey thoughts and images. What happened to me cannot be adequately written about. Our imaginations do not suffice, but I will use words because that is all we have.

After my two life-changing spiritual experiences I didn't tell anyone for years. I was afraid they would think I was crazy. Then in time, I realized God had given those experiences to me, not just for myself, but for everyone. I looked for a way to understand them as well as a language to speak about them to other people. After some time I came across a few books written by a medical doctor, Raymond Moody, who was a surgeon. The books I read were entitled *Life After Life* and *The Light Beyond*. In these books, Dr. Moody wrote about people who were undergoing operations who ran into difficulties. According to their vital signs they seemed to have died. They lost pulse and heartbeat. After several minutes, their vitals returned and when they awoke they had stories to tell. While the stories differed according to each person, there were many commonalities. These similar experiences happened to people of different races, gender and even religions. Doctor Moody termed what happened to these people near-death experiences, or N.D.E.'s. Here are the classic elements that people reported:

- The sensation of leaving the body
- The feeling of going through a tunnel
- An encounter with God/light
- A life review
- An understanding of being given more time and going back
- Memory of the event and a purposely changed life

Even though I wasn't on an operating table or even sick at the time, these classic elements of N.D.E. are the best way I've found to describe what happened to me. While I had two experiences a month apart from each other, they were so similar that I will speak of them here as one and the same. These both happened at the moment I went to bed and was drifting off to sleep.

Prior to these dramatic experiences I hadn't really had anything I would call a mystical or spiritual experience. I was young, I had been praying for wisdom, and I was seeking, asking, and knocking. Months and months went by as I hung on by simple faith. Suddenly, in one night, the words of Jesus became literally true in my life. I experienced a rebirth. When we are born we come out of a tunnel, our mother's womb. When I was reborn, I came through another tunnel, the passageway of transcendence and eternity. We don't change completely in an instant, but because of this experience my prior assumptive world and behaviors were shaken and I would never be the same.

Besides Dr. Moody's books, I want to point out the well-researched book, *Evidence of the Afterlife,* by Jeffrey Long, M.D. Written in 2010, this book is a scientific examination of thousands of NDE's. This book is fascinating reading. Dr. Long highlights that even blind people who have never seen can describe visual features from their NDE. He concludes, "I believe without a shadow of a doubt that there is life after physical death."

Wisdom Gained

It was through and because of prayer that these dramatic revolutionary experiences came to me. Solomon also attests: "Therefore I prayed, and understanding was given me; I called upon God, and the spirit of wisdom came to me." (Wis. 7:7)

When I called out for wisdom, God revealed many truths to me. I went from being a spiritual misfit to a mystic. These truths would alter my destiny and radically change my lifestyle. I discovered that God truly does hear the longings of our heart. My hunger for truth was great, and I urge you to get in touch with your hunger, your heart's desire. It comes from God. Let desire drive you forward and propel you to a deeper, more meaningful life.

> *God truly does hear the longings of our heart.*

I learned many truths about myself, and life itself, through these mystical experiences. Understanding was poured into my lap. First of all, I understood that things are not what they seem. We are very sensory-oriented people. We rely on our sight, hearing, and other senses. But, there is a lot more than meets the eye. God is the creator of the visible and the invisible. Besides being illusory, the world as we know it is passing away. But just beneath the surface of our temporal grasp lies a deep, permanent reality. Spiritual mystics call this the transcendent. Most people live a surface life and are oblivious to what is real. Spiritual people go beyond the natural to the supernatural. We all have the capability. Above all, we were created as spiritual beings. Pierre Teilhard de Chardin said, "We aren't physical beings having spiritual experiences. We are *spiritual* beings having a physical experience." I used to think I didn't have a spiritual side. These experiences awakened me to a whole new view of myself. I am spiritual first. My body isn't all of who I am, it is the dwelling place of God.

While it doesn't seem like anyone sees or hears us, God is well aware of our thoughts, imaginations, and motivations. "Behold the judge stands at the door!" (Jas. 5:9) That "door" is the door of your heart. Your conscience, too, is awake and active constantly, although we are not always in touch with, nor do we listen to, our deepest self.

After my spiritual awakening, as I was coming back to my ordinary consciousness, I told myself, "Remember, things are not what they seem. Just beneath the surface is a whole new reality. You must live an authentic life and not be deceived by your senses. Strive to commune with your truest self." I made an inner vow to live a deeper life. That is one of the main reasons I became not just a priest, but a monk. I treasure solitude and the exploration of my inner self. I try not to be tricked by the world and its enticements. "For all that is in the world, the lust of the flesh and the lust of the eyes and the pride of life, is not of the Father but is of the world." (1 Jn. 2:16) The way I try to get in touch with my deepest self is through meditation and contemplative prayer.

Psalm 131 is such a simple, precious psalm:

O Lord, my heart is not lifted up, my eyes are not raised too high; I do not occupy myself with things too great and too marvelous for me. But I have calmed and quieted my soul, like a child quieted at its mother's breast; like a child quieted is my soul.

Most people miss their truest self. They are too caught up in the world and its flashy allurements to ever delve deeper. Smart phones, computers, television, addictions, and the pursuit of money is like a fish hook with a worm on it for most people. Many find their sense of self in the way they look, their jobs, their roles as a parent, priest, or child. We are so much more than our circumstances dictate. The things of this world help build a false self. We must transcend this and find the face we were born with, apart from all the trappings. Blessed is the one who has the insight to go beyond these attractions and seeks who they really are apart from things and appearances. Jesus taught something very enigmatic and radical, "Whoever finds their life will lose it, and whoever loses their life for my sake will find it." (Mt. 10:39)

I love this quote by St. Augustine:

Men go abroad to wonder at the heights of mountains, at the huge waves of the sea, at the long courses of the rivers, at the vast compass of the ocean, at the circular motions of the stars, and they pass by themselves without wondering.

Give yourself credit. You have a deep spiritual side. Cultivate transcendence and depth. You will commune with your truest self. Nothing is easy in life, especially when it comes to your spiritual side. But challenges make champions. Spending time in quiet and exploring your deeper, inner life won't be easy. People have gone away to the desert and spent years upon years searching for the transcendent. Being a monk is a difficult life. Most people try silence and meditation and give up because they don't experience anything right away. But those who stand up to the challenge discover who they really are. If you cultivate quiet and solitude as a lifestyle you will find a wellspring of life within you that will become your foundation. You will come to know God in a personal way and you will find eternity in your heart. (Ecc. 3:11) Shakespeare wrote, "To thine own self be true." We are most true to ourselves when we embrace our spiritual side.

The Summons

I want to try to explain to you what happened to me. My near-death experiences happened right after I went to bed. I was drifting off to sleep, when suddenly I felt myself aware of being pulled toward God. We have a forgotten instinct within us that knows immediately where we are going, when this "pull" happens (The same thing will happen when we die. We will go to God). I remember fighting it and trying to wake up. I didn't want to go, but the force pulling me was too great and I had to surrender to it. I knew instinctively that I was going to God but I didn't want to face the immediacy of God's presence. As Scripture says, "It is a fearful thing to fall into the hands of the living God." (Heb. 10:31)

You might be thinking, "God loves us—why be afraid?" That's easy to think now, but trust me, when you are being summoned before his throne, the immediacy of the moment will have you terrified. Even Mary trembled in fear before the angel Gabriel.

I realized later that this wasn't some arbitrary spiritual experience. I was being summoned, asleep but fully conscious, and I was about to enter the throne room of the King of Kings and Lord of Lords. I was being summoned by Almighty God! I was about to stand before the creator of my life and be scrutinized and, as I later realized, invested with a call. Although I fought it and didn't want to go, I was powerless to resist. A force that was tremendously strong was drawing me there and I had no say in the matter.

The God Question

One question that had always plagued me from my youth was this, "Is there a God or not?" I reasoned if I could have the answer to any one question in life, it would be that one simple query. Once I knew the answer to the God question, I could then orient my life around its answer. I wondered, "Would it be possible to really know? Doesn't faith in God mean that you cling to hope without certainty? Does anyone really know?"

Is there a God or not?

In time I learned God gives revelation about himself to those who seek. The word "revelation" literally means "to pull back the curtain." For example, the book of Revelation is when God pulls back the curtain about the mystery of the end of the world and shows us what will happen. God also discloses the truth about himself by revelation. We can learn about God through books or even the Bible, but nothing suffices like first-hand knowledge. I love what Paul prayed:

May the God of our Lord Jesus Christ, the Father of glory, give you a spirit of wisdom and of *revelation* in the knowledge of him, having the eyes of your hearts enlightened...

(Eph. 1:17; italics added)

What a powerful prayer! Paul is praying that God would reveal himself to all of us and give us wisdom.

God is Light

When I came to the end of the tunnel I saw the light! "God is light and in him there is no darkness." (1 Jn. 1:5) In my experience, God revealed himself to me (and now to you through me.) I was not allowed to see God's form. No one can see the face of God and live. (Ex. 33:20) But what I did perceive was light brighter than the sun. It was similar to looking at the sun with your eyes closed. I was illumined from head to toe. The light shone through me and penetrated me. It was radiant and alive. I didn't just bask in this light, I was embraced by it; it warmed me and I felt total tranquility.

I was keenly aware of my smile. It was as though I could see myself smiling. I was in total bliss. Ps. 16:11 tells us, "In God's presence is the fullness of joy." I've been happy in life before but nothing like this. This was the joy of being loved, the ecstasy of being accepted, and the joy of being known. The feeling was one of rapture. You must understand, the whole time I was in God's presence, I was flooded with glory. God is glorious. Ps. 104:1 attests "God is robed in splendor and glory." What is glory? Glory is the apprehension of God's electric presence.

God's character and deeds are impeccable. He has existed from the beginning and is the creator of all things visible and invisible. God is almighty, he is victorious, and because of his virtue and deeds, God is glorious. This glory isn't only a spectacular appearance, it is a pleasurable, rapturous feeling. The only way to describe what I was experiencing was that wave upon wave of pleasurable electricity was flowing through my soul because I was having an audience with the King! Human kings wear crowns and flowing robes to make a dazzling appearance. When we see them we say, "Wow!" God's appearance isn't something you simply see. You become a participant in his splendor.

I was experiencing the beatific vision for which we are all made. I was tasting what will happen when we die. One day we will all go before God's glorious presence. The old adage is absolutely true: You will go back to your Maker. While I couldn't see anything but light, I reveled in the ecstasy and joy of God's presence. I was allowed time to soak it in. I will never forget the pure pleasure I felt. This glory, by the way, is what we feel when the Holy Spirit touches us. When you feel goosebumps, you have just a taste of the overwhelming glory you will feel when you stand before God's throne. As Isaiah wrote, we are created for God's glory. (Is. 43:7)

> *One day we will go before God's glorious presence.*

Our Face Before We Were Born

What I am about to write is hard to put into words and may be a bit controversial, theologically. But, it was my experience. When in God's presence I had the overwhelming sense and inner knowledge that I had been there before. Not only had I been there before but I was finally in touch with who I really am as I stood there. Somehow my life on earth was a "forgetting" and before God I was fully remembering who I really was. Now that I am back on earth I don't fully understand this because I have forgotten again. But I told myself to remember and not forget this important fact. Jesus seems to attest to this truth when he taught, "I know where I've come from and I know where I'm going." (Jn. 8:14)

Since my NDE's I have done some research about the preexistence of the soul. While not a well-known doctrine, some early church fathers such as Origen taught about near-death experiences. They were condemned by the Council of Constantinople in 553. I heard Fr. Richard Rohr say, "We forget the face we had before we were born." He was referring to our true self that we lose as we surround it with the trappings of this world. Our true self is who we are apart from our constructed persona and personality.

Whether approved by the church or not, I remembered that my soul preexisted and I have not forgotten this fact. It is now part of my own lifelong search for my truest self. William Wordsworth, in *Ode on Imitations of Immortality* wrote, "Our birth is but a sleep and a forgetting..." We have all heard that babies are not only innocent but know more about God when they are born than do adults. As we grow older, we forget.

In addition, I always thought God was out there somewhere. I felt he would remain distant so that faith would play its role. What I discovered is that space out there isn't the "final frontier" as proclaimed by Star Trek. Rather, it is our hearts that are the final frontier. I really believe the mysteries of the universe won't be revealed by the Hubble telescope but by searching within.

As Augustine so truthfully stated, "Our hearts are made for thee and our hearts are restless until they rest in thee." It is our hearts we must guard with all vigilance, for from the heart flow the issues of life. (Prov. 4:23) When referring to God's presence Jesus taught, "Out of your heart will flow rivers of living water." (Jn. 7:38) The secrets we seek lie within the core of our being. In *The Little Prince,* Antoine de Saint-Exupery expressed this wonderful truth: "And now here is my secret, a very simple secret: It is only with the heart that one can see rightly; what is essential is invisible to the eye."

God is far from being "out there." God is actually closer to us than we are to ourselves. Because God offers us a personal relationship with him, we are as close to God as we want to be. He is available to each of us.

The God question is one that confronts every person who is given life. Is there a God or not? And, if so, what does he require of me? God is faithful to reveal himself to each person as they authentically seek Him. Again, the revelation may not be dramatic, but there will come an inner knowing. This inner recognition is the beginning of eternal life.

Encountering God changes everything. Discovering the truth of God's reality was, and continues to be, revolutionizing for me. Now the question shifts from "Is there a God" to "What is it that God wants me to do?" I like Micah's explanation: "You have been told, O mortal, what is good. What does the Lord require of you? To act justly, love mercy and walk humbly with your God." (Mi. 6:8)

Judgment

The Scriptures teach "It is appointed to man to die once and then comes the judgment." (Heb. 9:27) This passage refutes the teaching of many that there is some sort of reincarnation. We die once, not over and over again.

As soon as we die, we have a life review. As I stood adoring God and soaking in his glory I was very aware of my unworthiness. I felt naked and exposed. There are numerous examples in the Bible explaining what I felt at that moment. Ps. 90:8 tells us, "Our secret sins lie exposed in the light of your face." When Isaiah had his vision of God's glory, he decried his unworthiness and said, "Woe is me! For I am lost and I have seen the King, the Lord of hosts!" When Jesus manifested his glory before Peter, Peter knelt down in the boat and said "Depart from me, for I am a sinful man O Lord." (Lk. 5:8) This feeling of unworthiness before the splendor of the Lord is known as "the fear of the Lord." This truth cannot be taught but is gift-given. When speaking about the judgment to come, Paul taught, "knowing the fear of the Lord, we persuade others." (2 Cor. 5:11)

I cannot put into words the feeling of standing before the awesome yet ravishing presence of God. The immediacy and intensity of the experience was overwhelming. Like heat from the sun, the radiance of God penetrated me. I was exposed and naked and there was nowhere to hide. Every thought and motivation I had ever had, every deed was scrutinized in an instant. I was an open book easily read. We have all heard people talk about "my life flashed before me in a moment." It is not so much God judges us as we judge ourselves in the light of perfection. I will do everything I can now to be right when I stand before the throne again at the end of my life. I have been given the gift of the fear of the Lord. I know I will return before God's throne and have to account for what I have done in the body. As Paul wrote: "Every one of us will have to appear before the judgment seat of Christ and account for what we have done, good or bad, in our bodies." (2 Cor. 5:10)

My life review revealed to me, beyond a shadow of a doubt, that I wasn't ready to die. I had nothing to show for my life. I was, as the Lord told me, not justified. The meaning of our life now is to be sure we are justified before God. Justification means that we are right with God. This happens in two main ways. First, we must receive forgiveness for our past wrongs and sins. This happens through the blood of Jesus on the cross. I've heard justification spoken of as "just as if" we had never sinned. As wonderful as God's mercy at the cross is, justification entails more.

We must also become just through virtue. We aren't made perfect at the cross, we are forgiven. The major work that God is doing in us is being justified. We are justified (forgiven) and we are being justified (being made holy) Another way to put this is "becoming the image of Jesus Christ."

Jesus was the first-born of many brothers and sisters. God's great plan and destiny for us is that we become like him. What was Jesus like? He was humble, forgiving, kind, merciful, forbearing, generous, patient, and loving. Jesus taught, "learn from me, for I am meek and humble of heart." (Mt. 11:29) In Catholic tradition we revere the sacred heart of Jesus. The goal of our life should be to be transformed into his image. That doesn't mean we look like Jesus physically, but morally, behaviorally, mentally, and spiritually. Perhaps the most

> *The goal of our life should be to be transformed into his image.*

important verse in the Bible that few reflect on is this: "For those whom God foreknew he also predestined to be *conformed to the image of his Son*, in order that he might be the first born among many brothers and sisters." (Ro. 8:29; italics added)

Are you ready for God's judgment? I wasn't. Thanks be to God, he gave me more time to get ready. I have received Jesus' death for me at the cross. I am now growing in virtue and developing my character. The next time I come before God I want to have something to show for my life. We don't earn salvation, we display the salvation given us by becoming like Christ. James said, "I, by my works, will show you my faith." (Ja. 2:18) At the judgment we will be standing shoulder to shoulder with people like Mother Teresa, Maximillian Kolbe, and Billy Graham. We must prove ourselves worthy of eternal life.

Passion and Purpose

Through these dramatic experiences I discovered the meaning of life. I have developed a trademark saying that came from my experiences with God, and I use it as the motto—and title—of my television program, *Live with Passion!* Passion is exuberance and energy. We can have passion in every area of our lives because life has meaning. There is purpose! Our purpose is to grow, help others, and please God.

As I've said before: focus on three main areas in your life. If you concentrate on these areas consistently, I believe you will be ready to meet God when you return to him:

- Develop your relationship with God as you journey. This happens predominantly through prayer, reading and learning, but also as you meet God in your daily life.

- Grow in character and virtue. Intentionally concentrate on becoming patient, generous, kind, and loving. These virtues are of infinite value! Also, examine yourself and turn away from vice, sin, and addictions. Be dedicated to fitness and personal well-being. Be committed to further learning and education.

- Make a difference! Have a cause and dedicate yourself to influencing people for good. You can't do everything, but you must do something. Through this cause you will exercise your gifts and come to realize your potential more fully.

Remember, who you are is God's gift to you. *Who you become* is your gift to God!

My near-death experiences reaffirmed for me that every new day we are given is magnificent and significant. Don't concentrate on and follow the lifestyles of those who are lost and have no purpose. The world is full of confused, lost, mediocre people who have no vision. We must separate ourselves from the wayward masses. We have a personal call from God:

You are a chosen race, a royal priesthood, a holy nation, God's own people, that you may declare the wonderful deeds of him who called you out of darkness into his marvelous light. Once you were no people but now you are God's people; once you had not received mercy but now you have received mercy. (1 Pet. 2:9-10)

A New Beginning

As young children we learn the truth that we will die. The unknown mystery of death and dying torments our human nature. What will the moment of death be like? Will there be a panicky feeling of suffocation as our life is snuffed out? Someone I know once told me, "I'm convinced that when we die there will only be blackness and nothing more."

Through my two near-death experiences I discovered, as our faith in Jesus proclaims, that death is not the end.

Rather, our death is a new beginning. Our souls are immortal. We have eternity in our hearts and we are made for forever. The moment of death is but a transition as we journey back to God, and we will be aware, awake and conscious of our return journey. God has a new life and resurrection prepared for us! God promises us a pain-free existence where there will be no more tears, and there will be a great reunion with our loved ones. The wealth of the nations will come upon us like an overflowing torrent. God will comfort us and the past will be forgotten. Peace will flow like a river. As Christians, we have a *living* hope.

I came across this story that in some ways illustrates what death can be like. A sick man was visiting his doctor and told him, "Doctor, I am afraid to die. I don't know what will happen and I fear it will an abrupt end. Do you know what lies on the other side? Is there another side?"

The Christian doctor was standing by a door. On the other side of the door was the sound of scratching and whining. Finally he opened the door. At that moment his dog sprang into the room tail wagging and jumping on his master with glee.

Turning to his patient the doctor said, "I've never allowed my dog to come into this examination room before. He didn't know what was in here. The only thing he knew was his master was inside. I don't know exactly what is on the other side of death, but I do know one thing. I know my Master is there and that is enough for me."

Our Master is in heaven and has prepared a place for us. Jesus is alive and will resurrect us.

Many have this reading from Job 19:25 proclaimed at their funeral service: "But as for me, I know my redeemer lives…" Similar to the dog in the story above, we know

Jesus lives and we will be united with him through our earthly death.

Be The Best!

When I was confirmed as a teenager we each choose a name to take as our confirmation name. I chose the name Jerome because I found the name in the front of our family Bible. The Bible was the St. Jerome edition of the Scriptures. Because of the near-death experiences I had, I should have taken the name Lazarus. Have you ever wondered what stories Lazarus would have told at the dinner he had with Jesus after he was raised from the dead? I believe the moral of my story—to be the best— is the same as his.

My life is a witness to the truth that because of Jesus Christ, we now have life after death! I prayed for wisdom as a young man and I was given much more than I ever thought I would, discerning a call from these revelations and becoming a Catholic priest. I also became a religious (a person who has taken monastic vows) and have professed vows of poverty, chastity, and obedience. I believe my vows and lifestyle help give credence to my words. I have no hidden agenda. I have no other motivation than to reveal the truths God has shared with me, and he has now given me a wonderful platform of writing, preaching, television, and radio to attest to these truths. I allowed the inevitability of my future death to change the way I was living.

The challenge of your upcoming death can make you a champion in life. Don't let death make you cower in fear, but let your unavoidable death inspire you to become the best you can be. Death challenges us to gain wisdom of heart and reach new heights in every area of life.

As I stood before God, I understood he was going to allow me to go back to my earthly life. I was allowed to communicate, and this is what I told God: "I will be the best!" I never forgot my statement. I have meditated upon my promise often and have allowed it to determine my life. My word to God has fueled my decisions and directed my energy throughout my life. I know I will one day return and I have made an inner vow to make my life extraordinary.

> *My word to God has fueled my decisions and directed my energy throughout my life.*

The story of these experiences is not just for me; now *you* are a part of my story. I believe with all my heart God foreknew my future ministry. When he summoned me he was giving me these experiences, not just for me, but for you! In an interactive way, you have had these near-death experiences by reading them here. They are now part of your imagination. I am praying that my promise (which I am now fulfilling) will be yours. *Be the best!*

When my dad was asleep, his passing came without warning and it was a total shock to all of us. I saw the doctor the next morning and he told me something interesting. He said, "There was no death struggle." What the doctor said told me dad didn't resist his death, but surrendered to it. He was being summoned home by God, and although he was only seventy-six years old, he didn't fight it.

In order to be ready for your death, I believe you must surrender to God now. Surrender is a lifestyle of seeking God, growing in character, and developing your potential. If you live a surrendered life, now you will be ready for death, your final surrender. Please pray with me now:

Lord, I treasure this magnificent gift of life. I want to live with you forever. I commit myself to developing my relationship with you. I will focus on growing in character. I will reach out and make a difference in the world. I give you my heart and my life now. Fill me with passion and purpose. May my life be significant and influential. Form me into the image of your Son, Jesus. I surrender all to you now. I will be the best! I believe I will live with you forever. Amen.

5
THE CHALLENGE OF RELATIONSHIPS

In June 2014, I was visiting my mother a few months before she died. I would always take her to Mass at the church in Florida that is staffed by the Redemptorist priests. They know me at Sacred Heart Church because I have preached two missions there. The Saturday night vigil Mass we attended was the Solemnity of the Most Holy Trinity. As we sat in the pew several minutes before Mass, praying, one of the staff members recognized me and came over to me with a strange look on his face. "Father, the priest hasn't shown up for Mass. Would you preside?"

It was ten minutes before Mass was to begin and my mind was racing. What would I say? There were hundreds of people gathering. Usually I begin my homily a week ahead of time and I pride myself on being prepared. Now I had to do something impromptu and off the cuff. I quickly organized my thoughts based on the Scriptures I know so well.

I re-introduced myself to the community. My mother was surprised to see me up there because she didn't overhear what had happened before Mass. My mind was still working as the readings were being proclaimed. Finally, I got up and proclaimed the familiar passage from John 3:16-18:

> For God so loved the world that he gave his only Son, so that everyone who believes in him may not perish but might have eternal life. For God

did not send his son into the world to condemn the world, but that the world might be saved through him. Whoever believes in him will not be condemned, but whoever does not believe has already been condemned, because they have not believed in the name of the only Son of God.

I began by telling the congregation how I had just been asked to preside out of the blue. People laughed when I told them I had ten minutes to prepare. I then launched into my homily. What I write here emerged from my homily that day.

My television program, *Live with Passion!*, now airs in many countries throughout the world on the Trinity Broadcasting Network (TBN) and the Church Channel. The reason I felt called to be on TV was because I wanted to proclaim God's love so that everyone can have a personal relationship with God. There are so many people who aren't going to church, who have fallen away, and who don't know God. As a Christian and Catholic priest I want to reach out to them! We can't expect them to come to church, we have to go to them. That is the genius of television. It takes the message of salvation beyond the walls of the church.

> There are so many people who aren't going to church, who have fallen away, and who don't know God.

On television, I want to inspire people to become their best and live their lives with passion. I want to encourage people to grow in God so they can realize their potential. But the number one reason I produce and air programs is because I want people to have eternal life. I have dedicated many programs explicitly toward the message of salvation.

St. Paul of the Cross, the founder of the Passionists, lived in the 1700's. He was a dynamic preacher and retreat leader. His nickname was "the hunter of souls." A priest's role is to inspire and encourage, but most of all to hunt for souls. We must bring people something that will endure, and put them in touch with the ultimate. We don't help people if we just teach them about this life. This life is tremendously significant, but time-wise, our life span is equivalent to only one grain of sand on all the beaches of the world. My call is to bring people to salvation, to eternal life. Proclaiming the salvation that is in Jesus is the main reason I preach, write, and produce for television and radio.

Eternal life is a phrase that appears many times in the Gospel of John. It has both a quantitative and qualitative meaning. First, it refers to life that will last forever. But it also refers to a new *quality* of life—God's life (the word is Zoe in the Greek). The life God possesses is rich and abundant. Within this life there is joy, peace and inner well-being. Tasting God's life is what Jesus meant when he said you must be born from above (or again). This eternal life begins not when we die, but when we believe in Jesus as Lord and Savior. You receive the Holy Spirit and begin a relationship with God on a whole new level. It is a personal relationship with God. Just because people go to church doesn't mean they have this relationship. Many simply have a ritualistic religion that appeases their guilt. But God calls us to so much more. That is why Pope Francis, in his apostolic exhortation, *The Joy of the Gospel* (#3) wrote,

> I invite all Christians, everywhere, at this very moment, to a renewed personal encounter with Jesus Christ, or at least an openness to letting

him encounter them…. No one should think this invitation is not for him or her.

Salvation means believing Jesus suffered and died for your sins. It means coming to know God *personally* and it includes developing a relationship with the Holy Spirit. When you come into a relationship with the Holy Spirit, eternal life has begun and continues when you die.

The Gospel tells us God *so loves* us. We see the scope of God's love when we read that he gave up his only Son for us. God is love. Love is God's nature, who God is. Love isn't something God does, it is a part of his character. God is loving, and it is love's nature to give. Love is generous and doesn't count the cost, and God has given us the greatest gift ever given: Jesus.

In this famous Gospel passage from John chapter three, which Martin Luther termed, "the Gospel in miniature," we hear that God loves *the world*. Right now there are over seven billion people on the face of the earth. It is easy to feel insignificant by the sheer enormity of that figure. I live in Houston, the fourth largest city in the U.S. There are so many people on the roads, in malls, and in restaurants. When I fly, people crowd airports and pack planes. Even though there are throngs of people everywhere, God pays attention to you. He knows you personally. Before you were born he had you in mind and called you into being. As we are told in Psalm 139, it was God who knit you together in your mother's womb. You didn't arbitrarily come to be by chance or even by your parents' willing it. God purposely created you.

The book I wrote prior to this one is titled, *You Are Loved!* In this important book I try to mediate an experience of God's love to people. I write about the fact that we are all unique, special and one of a kind. We all have unique fingerprints and an individualized DNA. Even if you have an identical twin, that person is not exactly like you. You are rare and different.

God so loved you, he sent his son for you. In fact, God is in love with *you*. Years ago, I attended a retreat where the leader spoke about John 3:16, which states, "For God so loved the world that he gave his only Son..." He suggested instead of using the word "world," at that moment we should place in our own name. For God so loved Mary, John, Jim, Andrew, Elizabeth, Cathy, you, and me. We need to personalize the Gospel and take it personally. God's love is unconditional, passionate, sacrificial, and deeply personally. More than anything, the feast of the Trinity proclaims salvation and God's love for us. I am praying that my books and TV productions will bring you into a saving relationship with the living God. I want you to have eternal life.

Whether you feel it or not right now, simply believe in the love God has for you. (1 Jn. 4:16) I am so inspired by this prayer penned by the apostle Paul:

> I bow my knees before the Father, from whom every family in heaven and on earth is named, that according to the riches of his glory he may grant you to be strengthened with might through his Spirit in your inner person, and that Christ may dwell in your hearts through faith; *that you, being rooted and grounded in love, may have power to comprehend with all the saints what is the breadth and length and height and depth, and to know the love of Christ which surpasses knowledge*, that you may be filled with all the fullness of God.
>   (Eph. 3:14-19; emphasis added)

Who Is God?

There are three readings for the Solemnity of the Trinity. One was the Gospel passage above, and the first reading came from Exodus 34:4-6

> Having come down in a cloud, the Lord stood with Moses there and proclaimed his name, LORD. Thus the Lord passed before him and cried out, "The Lord, the Lord, a merciful and gracious God, slow to anger and rich in kindness and fidelity.

I travel to various churches all over the U.S. and Canada, preaching missions. The goal of these missions is for people to deepen their relationship with God. I want them to have the assurance of salvation and to live lives of passion. As I encounter people everywhere, I see first-hand that people are in need of healing. People need healing in their relationships and wounded emotions.

> *The goal of these missions is for people to deepen their relationship with God.*

Sometimes we celebrate the sacrament of the sick because people are hurting physically. People also need inner healing. They could be living in fear and dread or be anxious all the time. Others feel guilty and need peace from self-recrimination. But perhaps the area of inner turmoil where people most need healing (and this cuts across all denominations) is their image of God.

So many live with a harsh and stern image of God. Perhaps they may not think of God that way consciously, but that picture of God is somehow buried in their subconscious. Some see God as an old man with a long, gray beard who sits on a throne watching us closely. To them, God is the "man in the sky." Others sense the Lord is an angry God, out to find fault—a computer in the sky with a ledger of all of our misdeeds. When it comes to this image of God, you'd better not make a false move or you will be punished.

Jonathan Edwards had his church in Northampton, Massachusetts, in the 1700's. He once preached a scorching sermon titled, "Sinners in the Hands of an Angry God." Most people have a vague feeling that God is mad at them, but the readings for the Solemnity of the Trinity tell us otherwise: God isn't mad *at* us but mad *about* us!

In my television programs I try to be very careful in how I portray God. For example, I remember in some movies God's voice is depicted as loud and mean. Granted, the Lord's voice flashes flames of fire. (Ps. 29:7) But it is also a "still, small voice." (1 Kg. 19:12) When Moses heard God call out of the burning bush, what type of voice did he hear? Was it a mean, stern voice or a gentle sound? In the movies we are used to hearing the loud authoritative voice of an actor such as James Earl Jones depicting God's voice. When I personify the voice of God in my teaching, I am careful to be sure I am soft and gentle in tone. There are several ways I could represent God's voice. Being harsh and loud is a big turn-off. This is one reason I use a female voice at the end of my programs, in order to give my episodes a softer tone. I believe we attract people by showing God's softer side.

In addition, I use supplementary media or B-roll in my productions. An example of this is when I am talking about a golf course and suddenly you see a lush golf course on the TV screen. We use previously shot footage and edit it in as I refer to certain things in order to help spark the imagination of the viewer. When I talk about

God, I have made it very clear to my producer to be careful what kind of B-roll he uses. In the past, he has gone with the traditional views of God that are masculine and stereotypically harsh. Or perhaps I will be talking about Jesus and he will show some kind of syrupy Jesus or cartoonish figure. I have had him do away with all that.

People need a good image of who God and Jesus are. My producer now uses images such as light, or shots of the universe or majestic mountains when I refer to God. There could be tender scenes like flowers or sunsets. For Jesus, we try to use images people can relate to, not a plastic Jesus. Perhaps it will be a hand extended toward you, or the scene might show two people hugging. Besides my preaching on the programs I am trying to help people have a better image of who God and Jesus are through television. Portraying God and Jesus in a positive light is extremely important to me.

We are used to hearing about wars and bloodshed and the God who exacts a life for a life, an eye for an eye and a tooth for a tooth. But in this reading we hear of a God who is merciful and gracious. God reveals himself as slow to anger, rich in kindness and fidelity. God shows himself to Moses as a God who is on our side and wants us to live and prosper. As Paul would later write, "If God is for us, who can be against us?" (Ro. 8:31)

The predominant image Jesus used for God was that of a father. In fact, he went beyond this and used the Aramaic word for familiarity and closeness: Abba. By using Abba, Jesus called God "daddy" or "papa." A father is one who creates and gives life to us. Fathers are masculine, strong and protective.

Many who are incarcerated lack a father figure. They come from broken homes where their father either died or abandoned the family. They list the lack of a father figure as the major contributing factor toward their breaking the law. We each need a father in our life. Jesus said, "I am going to my father and *your father...*" (Jn. 20:17) Just as God was a father to Jesus, he is a father to us. When he taught us to pray Jesus told us to begin, "Our father..." (Mt. 6:9)

I'm so glad I had a good father figure. Having a gracious father on earth has helped me to view God in a positive manner. My father cared for me and loved me. I always called my father "dad" because we had an intimate relationship. We were close emotionally and shared life together. My dad was my best friend. I could tell him everything. When he used "Abba," Jesus was telling us that God isn't simply our creator, but the One who walks closely with us and cares deeply about us.

But God is beyond being masculine. The prophet Isaiah wrote these stirring lines:

Can a mother forget the baby at her breast and have no compassion on the child of her womb? Even if a mother could forget her baby, I will not forget you. (Is. 49:15)

The prophet was telling us that we always have God's attention. Like a mother who watches over her baby, God watches over us. God has the stereotypic feminine qualities. Mothers are tender, soft and gentle and extremely solicitous of their young. Isaiah is hinting that God has this feminine quality, also. When some talk about God they use philosophical terms such as the ground of our being, or being itself. To me, that depersonalizes God. Yes, existentially God proclaimed his name as the great "I Am." God is a being, yes, but God is so much more. God is existence itself, possessing both masculine and feminine characteristics.

The late, well-known priest Henri Nouwen wrote a book called, *The Return of the Prodigal*. In this book he referred to Rembrandt's famous painting, *The Return of the Prodigal*. In the painting, Rembrandt captured the moment when the rebellious son returned to his father. As he kneels before his father in contrition, the father reaches out both arms and places his hands on each shoulder. The father is hugging his child, ecstatic that he has his son back safe and sound. Nouwen points out something interesting about the hands of the father. The left hand is different in size and appearance from the right. The left is larger and more masculine looking. The right is smaller and softer in appearance. He has an interesting interpretation about this discrepancy. God is both masculine and feminine in his qualities. While he has the characteristics of a father that are strong, protective and powerful, the Father also has the motherly qualities of being soft, tender and caring. God is certainly all this and more.

Whenever I used to hear people praying to God as "she" it would throw me. Now I am not so jarred when I hear this. In my formation I was taught to be inclusive when I use language. Instead of always referring to God as male, I try to find other words to describe God as He truly is. While God is a person, Jesus taught that God is a spirit. He is more than masculine or feminine; these are categories derived by humans. While God has the best of the qualities of both, we must go beyond those understandings when describing him.

I heard a story about a second grade class. The teacher wanted them to use their imaginations and draw pictures of anything they wanted. They would then display these pictures and talk about them with the others in the class. After ten minutes or so, she began to walk around and observe what each student was working on. When she came to little Mary she said, "What are you drawing?" She replied, "I'm making a picture of God." "Well honey, no one knows what God looks like," said the teacher. The little girl replied, "They will when I'm finished!"

In many churches a preacher will say, "God is good," and the people will automatically reply, "All the time." Then the preacher will say, "All the time…" and the people respond, "God is good!" The picture the Scriptures paint about God is one who is kind, slow to anger, and merciful. Jesus spoke to St. Faustina and said, "My mercy is greater

> *God is good…*
> *All the time!*
>
> *All the time…*
> *God is good!*

than all of your sins and all of the sins of the *whole world!*" God's benevolent image is a consistent portrait presented to us time and time again in the Bible. Jesus attests to the truth of God's goodness by telling us God is approachable and accessible.

Not Good to be Alone

The final Scripture presented to us on the feast of the Trinity has to do with the nature of the Trinity. God is one, yet three, persons. It included this important verse: "The grace of the Lord Jesus Christ and the love of God and the fellowship of the Holy Spirit be with all of you." (2 Cor. 13:14)

We begin each Mass using this verse as our greeting. After the music and the sign of the cross, the presider greets the people, not with the cultural "hello" or "good morning," but with this faith statement. The new missal has changed the words a little to be: "The grace of the Lord Jesus Christ and the love of God and the *communion* of the Holy Spirit be with you all." (2 Corinthians 13:14; italics added)

Priests greet people at Mass with our understanding of God. We also greet people with our hope. We pray that you would receive grace, know God's love, and have communion with God in the Holy Spirit. This greeting proclaims that God is relational himself, and desires a relationship with us. Actually, the Mass itself is a prayer. At Mass, we pray *to* the Father, *through* the Son, *in* the Holy Spirit.

It is interesting that, although the concept of trinity is embraced by most Christian denominations, the word "trinity" isn't found in the Bible. But the notion of trinity is found in many places in the Bible. This sentiment is how Paul concludes his long letter to the church at Corinth. Another familiar Scripture that highlights the truth of the Trinity is: "Go and make disciples of all nations, baptizing them in the name of the Father and of the Son and of the Holy Spirit." (Mt. 28:19)

In this important verse we are told to baptize people in the name of our Trinitarian God. When you are baptized you aren't baptized in the name of "God" but in the name of all three persons of God. We don't have to be a Scripture scholar or liturgist to understand what Jesus is saying here. God is a Trinity of persons.

Another verse that has classically been understood as Trinitarian is: "Let us make humanity in our own image, in our own likeness…" (Gen. 1:26)

Pay attention to the words "us" and "our" in this verse. This Scripture shows God is speaking of himself as being plural. The general interpretation has been this verse is a reference to God's nature as the Trinity. Since we are made in his image, we are a tripartite being. Humans are body, soul, and spirit. (1 Thess. 5:23)

One other Trinitarian verse I want to point out is Isaiah 6:8, which says, "Who will go for *us*?" (italics mine)

This reference is the call of Isaiah to be a prophet. As with my near-death experiences, Isaiah is summoned into the throne room of God. He experiences God's glory and encounters the Lord. Isaiah is allowed to see God to some degree. He also hears the angels singing. We use the words of the angels in the order of the Mass at the conclusion of the Preface as we pray and sing "Holy, Holy, Holy Lord God of hosts. Heaven and earth are full of your glory. Hosanna in the highest." The thrice-holy adoration by the angels is perhaps yet another allusion to the Trinity.

In this vision, Isaiah receives a call and is commissioned by God to go and speak to the people. Once again, God speaks of himself in the plural as he refers to himself as "us."

Besides the witness of the Scriptures, the doctrine of the Trinity was first proposed by the Church father, Tertullian, in the early 200's. The summary of his position was Father, Son and Spirit are one in essence—the three persons are distinct, but of one substance or nature. They are three beings and have three different functions. The Father is the Creator, the Son is the Redeemer and the Spirit is the Sanctifier. The Nicene Creed is Trinitarian. When we pray the creed we pray,

I believe in one God, the Father Almighty…I believe in one Lord Jesus Christ, the Only Begotten Son of God…begotten, not made, consubstantial with the Father…I believe in the Holy Spirit, the Lord, the giver of life, who proceeds from the Father and the Son…

We are all familiar with the concept of the Trinity, and much has been written about the Trinity in theology. While it is hard to understand all the subtleties and ramifications, we must accept the witness of the Scripture, and tradition, as fact. God is a Trinity of persons.

The word "trinity" has become common to our modern life. For example, my television program airs on the largest Christian network in the world: The Trinity Broadcasting Network. Its founders, Paul and Jan Crouch, wanted to honor the holy Trinity by giving the network this name. Countless lives have been saved and touched by this media outreach, all in the name of the Trinity. Additionally, there is Trinity College in Connecticut. Other cities and countries in the world have schools named after the Trinity, and some of you may belong to a local church named after the Trinity.

Much ink has been spilled trying to determine precisely how it is that Jesus is both human and divine. What did he know or not know? Even more volumes have been written about the make-up and mix of the three persons of the Trinity. Great saints, theologians and doctors of the church have waxed eloquently and forcefully about the doctrine of the Trinity. Revered figures such as Augustine, Bonaventure, and Aquinas have written extensively about this truth. Church councils such as the Council of Nicea, the source of the Nicene Creed, have formulated pronouncements about the Trinity. Great minds have wrestled with this and tradition has much to say.

Even after the plentitude of information that has been formulated and processed, questions remain. How can they be three persons and yet one God? How can they be independent and yet have one mind and will? There are many questions still to be answered and much remains a mystery.

> *How can they be three persons and yet one God?*

The Catholic Catechism reveals truth about our understanding of the Trinity:

> The mystery of the Most Holy Trinity is the central mystery of Christian faith and life. It is the mystery of God in himself. It is therefore the source of all the other mysteries of faith, the light that enlightens them. It is the most fundamental and essential teaching in the "hierarchy of the truths of faith". The whole history of salvation is identical with the history of the way and the means by which the one true God, Father, Son, and Holy Spirit, reveals himself to men "and reconciles and unites with himself those who turn away from sin.
>
> (#234)

The Trinity is a mystery of faith in the strict sense, one of the "mysteries that are hidden in God, which can never be known unless they are revealed by God". To be sure, God has left traces of his Trinitarian being in his work of creation and in his revelation throughout the Old Testament. But his inmost Being as Holy Trinity is a mystery that is inaccessible to reason alone, or even to

Israel's faith before the Incarnation of God's Son and the sending of the Holy Spirit. (*#237*)

Images

Images help me when I try to grasp the concept of the Trinity in my own thoughts. As humans we are body, soul and spirit. While each part that comprises who we are is different in function, they all work together to give us life and make us fully human. Many denominations of Christians pray in the name of the Father and of the Son and of the Holy Spirit. We Catholics make the sign of the cross over us as we pray those words. The sign of the cross is Trinitarian.

St. Patrick is said to have explained the Trinity by using the metaphor of a shamrock. A shamrock is a little green clover found in Ireland. It has one main stem and three leaves growing off of the center. The three leaves form one complete shamrock. Another example of the concept of the Trinity is a beam of light pouring through a window. Within that beam of light is heat, light, and energy, yet it is one beam. The functions and qualities differ, but the ray of light is one. These examples mostly explain functions, but not the distinction of intelligence and will that exist between the persons of the Godhead. Those are distinctions that remain a mystery.

The Trinity doesn't simply exist as three persons in one God. Each person of God relates to the other, making the Trinity relational. The Father loves the Son and the Son the Father. (Jn. 15:9) Jesus taught, "All that belongs to the Father is mine. The Spirit will tell you whatever he receives from me." (Jn. 16:15) Jesus prayed that we would all be one as he and the Father are one. (Jn. 17:21) There is an intimate commingling between the persons of God, a deep, profound sharing of each person in the Trinity. There is unity and agreement of will and intelligence.

John of Damascus talked about the *interpenetration* between the persons of the Trinity. The word in the Greek that attempts to describe this mysterious relationship is "perichresis," which means a symbiotic rotation between the three persons.

St. Bernard of Clairvaux was a great mystic and proponent of contemplative, or centering, prayer. It is in centering prayer that we can unite our wills, imaginations, and hearts to God. We become divinized by receiving the Holy Spirit, but also as our wills are united to God's in prayer. St. Bernard taught that the Holy Spirit isn't generated, but processes from, the love of the Father and the Son through an act of their unified will. He spoke of the Spirit as being God's kiss.

> If, as is properly understood, the Father is he who kisses, the Son he who is kissed, then it cannot be wrong to see in the kiss the Holy Spirit, for he is the imperturbable peace of the Father and the Son, their unshakable bond, their undivided love, their indivisible unity. — St. Bernard of Clairvaux, in Sermon 8, *Sermons on the Song of Songs*

We need to have some sort of intellectual grasp of the Trinity, but the danger is to get into endless speculation. I don't need to know all of the subtleties. I have studied the Scriptures, read the saints, and reasoned within. I believe the testimony of tradition.

While the doctrine of the Trinity may sound absurd to some, I have accepted it as a revealed mystery. I've come to the conclusion that the *Trinity isn't a mystery to be solved or even fully understood, but a relationship to be entered into*! God is relationship and he invites us into a personal relationship with him—something intimate and extremely subjective. While it may have similar aspects from person to person, this relationship will always be unique and individualistic.

St. Therese of the Little Flower talked about her "little way." She was very humble and didn't aspire to greatness, but loved God deeply. Although she lived communally and prayed together in common, she was an individual and different from everyone else. She had her own humility and approach to God. God loved her uniqueness and her way of worship and reverence. Similarly, when it comes to God, you must be yourself. Yes, learn techniques and methods of prayer. Pray with the church communally. But most of all, don't let go of who you are. Approach God in your own, unique little way. God made you who you are. Why try to pray like others? Learn from others, certainly, but don't be exactly like them.

We all have a little way.

God wants a relationship with you, not with someone else who prays in such-and-such-a-way for however long. No one can love God exactly like you. You are unique, different, and one of a kind. Don't lose your precious individuality. Love God like no one else ever has! Through your own way of praying you will develop something unique with God that no one has ever had. Show God who you really are and what kind of a lover you can be.

We were created to be related to God and others. John Donne wrote: "No man is an island, entire of itself, every man is a piece of the continent, a part of the main."

And in Genesis 2:18 we hear God say, "It is not good for man to be alone."

Father, Son and Spirit

My prayer life has taken many forms throughout the years, but one truth has remained consistently. My prayer toward God is Trinitarian. Since God is Father, Son, and Spirit, in order to have a personal relationship with God, you should have a personal relationship with each person of the Trinity. Sometimes I find myself praying to the Father. Other times I come before Jesus. In contemplative or centering prayer, I concentrate on the Holy Spirit. In the morning, I make sure I pray to all three persons of God. At various times throughout the day we can pray to each of the persons of the Trinity. Hopefully, you are able to relate to each person. Praying in a Trinitarian fashion expands and enriches your prayer life.

Jesus taught, "When you pray, go to your room, close the door and pray to your Father who is in secret. Your Father who sees you in secret will reward you." (Mt. 6:6) God is your creator and the one who has sustained you during your entire life thus far. Since I had a good father figure on earth, I relate to God as father easily. My father and I were best friends and I knew I could trust him completely. Even if you didn't have a good father figure, I believe you can relate to God as your father. If you were abused by your father or disregarded by him, pray for healing and the restoration of trust. A powerful verse is, "Even though my father and mother forsake me, the Lord will receive me." (Ps. 27:10)

Jesus constantly taught, "come to me." (Mt. 11:28) Jesus is our Master, our teacher, our friend. He was fully human and completely understands what we go through.

When we encounter times of stress, anxiety, fear, and grieving, we can come to him for support. He will never fail or forsake us. Jesus is closer to us than a brother. He is the Good Shepherd who is concerned about us and watches over us. One word the Scriptures use for Jesus is Emmanuel. This name from the prophet Isaiah means "God with us." Jesus is commonly referred to as Emmanuel at Christmas time, and during Advent we sing "O Come O Come Emmanuel." I wrote the sentiment below as I celebrated Christmas one year:

> What difference does Jesus make? *What a difference* Jesus makes! Because Jesus is with me, I can:
>
> Grieve well. Face the future. Let go of the past. Deal with difficult people. Live with peace. Have hope. Be strong. Face my challenges. Live with purpose and meaning. Forgive and live. Be spiritual. Love myself. Live with Passion! Realize my potential. Experience rebirth. Change, grow and become. Make a difference. Love others.
>
> What a difference Jesus makes!

Some have a problem with a Father image or even a masculine image such as Jesus. Within the Trinity we have a feminine image for God: Sophia. Sophia is the Greek word for wisdom and is often applied to the Holy Spirit. In the book of Wisdom, God's Spirit is spoken of as "she." (Wis. 6:12-17) While all-powerful and fierce, I've found the Spirit of God is gentle, tender, and very loving. The Holy Spirit is kind and ever-present. The Spirit comes to help us. We don't know how to pray as we ought, and the Spirit even helps us to pray. (Ro. 8:26) God's Spirit lives in us and invites us to communion. We begin Mass with "the communion of the Holy Spirit be with you all." The communion we are invited to is to know God personally.

Our prayer life can and should be Trinitarian. We ought to develop a relationship with each person of the Trinity. At various times we will pray to one or the other of the persons of God. You may find yourself giving more time to the Holy Spirit or Jesus. Other seasons of your life may find you focusing on God the Father. In my morning prayer I always begin by praising and then speaking to the Father. Then I address Jesus. I conclude by worshipping and praying to the Holy Spirit. Throughout the day I come before one or another person of the Trinity, depending on how I am moved or what of my needs may be.

I hardly ever pray "God." That word is too impersonal for me. I always focus on one person of the Trinity or sometimes pray, "Father, Son, and Spirit." The fascinating truth is, when you pray to one person of the Trinity, you are relating to all three, for they are inseparable. Rather than just praying to an impersonal God, try being more precise and focused by addressing God as a Trinity of persons. My favorite quote from St. Francis of Assisi regarding God is: *"My God and my All!"* God the Father, Son, and Spirit is truly our *all*.

From the beginning, God predestined us to be his adopted sons and daughters. We are invited into a familial and familiar relationship with him. Just as God is a relationship of persons and we are made in his image, we are invited into this communion of persons. Since we have been divinized by the Holy Spirit, we are summoned to become one with God and know him deeply and personally. One day we will know completely, even as we are known. (1 Cor. 13:12). God honors us by drawing us into his very union of persons.

One of my favorite places is the Camadolese monastery just South of Big Sur, California. The Camadolese are a religious community of monks and nuns who are part of the Benedictine monastic tradition. They spend large amounts of time seeking God and communing with God in contemplative prayer. Their monastery is perched on the side of a mountain about 1,400 feet high, overlooking the Pacific Ocean. The views are striking and stunning. At night it is so dark, thousands of twinkling stars can be seen with the naked eye. In the middle of the night I've even seen the white milk of the Milky Way.

As you enter the doors into their chapel, the first thing you see is an icon by the Russian artist Andrei Rublev from the early 1400's. It shows the three angels who appeared to Abraham, seated around a square table. They are blessing the chalice on the table, which is a symbol of the Eucharist. As the observer looks at the icon the nearest place at table is unoccupied and available. That place is for you and me.

Jesus said, "Behold, I stand at the door and knock; If any one hears my voice and opens the door, I will come in to that one and eat with them and they with me." (Rev. 3:20) To eat with someone in the Semitic world meant intimacy and closeness. This icon symbolically proclaims the invitation to intimacy given to you and me by the three persons of the Trinity.

> *Behold, I stand at the door and knock.*

When I went to Mass that Trinity Sunday with my Mom, I wasn't prepared to preside. I was suddenly asked to preside and preach. That challenge brought out some of the best in me, and my homily took on a life of its own. My reflections that day turned into an episode of one of my television programs, and then turned into this reflection on the Trinity. Glory to the Father and to the Son and to the Holy Spirit!

Created to be Related

We are created to be related. We are made in the image of God, who is a Trinitarian relationship and desires to live with us forever. But God also created us to relate to others. We are born connected to our mother by an umbilical cord and become a member of a family. Some of us live in religious communities. We are members of parishes, denominations, neighborhoods, cities and countries. God gave us the gift of language so that we could build relationships with each other. As God mused in the beginning, "It is not good for man to be alone…"

Anthropologists and psychologists have done studies with monkeys who were isolated right after birth. Those monkeys grow up maladjusted and never become part of the group. We need nurturing and socialization in order to become well-adjusted and contribute to society. We need some degree of love from our parents, family, and friends to achieve well-being.

As I am writing this, Pope Francis has called for a Synod on family life. This extraordinary Synod of bishops began with an initial gathering in October 2014. It will conclude with a general synod in October 2015 "for the good of the families, church and society." In this assembly, bishops from around the world voiced their opinions on controversial issues such as same-sex marriages and cohabitation. As I write this, questions are circulating to many about family life. They are asked to answer these questions in order to give input to our leaders. The bishops will take this input and produce guidelines. The complete name of the synod is "The Vocation and Mission of the Family in the Church and in the Contemporary World." For too long, the church has been criticized for being irrelevant and out of touch with where most people live. The preliminary work and meetings will help the leaders of the Church get in touch with family life and make clear, relevant pronouncements.

I am the youngest of three children. I always got along well with my parents; in fact, I felt favored over my sisters by both of them. I learned a lot about accepting others as they are, as well as how to forgive, from dealing with my sisters. My middle sister and I struggled with relating to each other. Anything I said she would take the wrong way. I misunderstood her moods. My older sister is a Jehovah's Witness and we cannot discuss religion or it results in an argument. Both have wonderful qualities and are very much people-persons; however, I struggle on various levels with each, and I try to keep the lines of communication open since we live a thousand miles apart. My mother's death brought us together and amid the tension we got along well. There are continuing challenges as we sell Mom's house and possessions. Some of you have been through this chore and you know the turmoil.

The challenge of relationships is to love, forgive, keep communicating, and accept others as they are. Difficult people can tease virtue out of us. This is part of our "becoming." Everyone wants to be a forgiving person, but when difficult people come into our lives, all of a sudden we find out just how hard it is to be virtuous. Having vowed myself to a religious community, I live in close quarters with people of different ethnicities and backgrounds. The ideal of community is "they were of one mind and heart." (Acts 4:32) The reality simply isn't so harmonious.

After evening prayer, many in our community of ten gather to watch the national news. Whenever anything political is shown, political commentary emerges from some people. I've discovered that I am in the minority on many issues. I want to watch the news, not get into tense arguments with others whose opinions can't be changed. The same people with whom I just prayed and wished the sign of peace can quickly become opinionated and argumentative. Others are quite gentle and aren't as forceful when it comes to their views and opinions.

Community stretches me and forces me to confront myself with how I want to behave. Living in a community forces me to evaluate my goals regarding others. I have to ask myself who I am and who I want to become when living with others. I've decided I want to forgive and accept others as they are, yet not compromise who I am at all costs.

As I live community life now and remember the family life I came from, I realize people are talented, gifted and blessed. But people have their own way of approaching life, and relationships can be messy because everyone has their own ideas and they differ from ours. Even when we think we are communicating clearly, we can be easily misunderstood. We can be touchy and easily offended. Usually, people don't mean to hurt us, but they do. They don't always agree with our views religiously, politically, or otherwise. We have to accept them as they are and agree to disagree. We all come from various backgrounds. Some are opinionated, controlling, contentious, abrupt, angry, aggressive, not passionate enough, moody, and offensive. Others are gentle, friendly and supportive.

I find accepting people the way they are and not taking their negative behavior personally is one of the best things one can do.

Relationships challenge us to become our best. There will always be people we get along with easily and enjoy; friendships are one of the greatest pleasures of life. Friends support us and help us in our journey. God always gives us people we can laugh with easily, but I've heard it said there will always be ten percent of people who, for whatever reason, don't like us. You must accept this truth and realize you can't hit it off with everyone. We all want to be liked and admired, but some will resist us. The temptation is to take offense and let others' opinions make you bitter and resentful. It is easy to become angry and aloof. Try not to blow things out of proportion. Don't let the negativity of others determine who you are and the way you respond.

One of the keys to having good, solid relationships is communication. When a marriage struggles, there is usually some sort of a communication breakdown. During a wedding ceremony, many like to symbolize their new oneness by lighting a unity candle. The bride and groom each hold a lit candle and, using their candles, at the same time they light a larger, solitary candle. Then something significant happens. Each blows out their candle. That extinguishing of their own candle is a powerful moment because it symbolizes that "self" must die in order for the two to become one. When you communicate, sometimes you have to let go of being right in order to make things work.

> *One of the keys to having good, solid relationships is communication.*

I am big on communicating. I reach out to tens of thousands of people weekly. Social media is an important means of communication. Since the early 1990's I have created and maintained a website. (Visit www.frcedric.org) Through this website people can request prayer. The Internet is one way people can contact me so that I can pray for their intentions. I have a Facebook page with a few thousand people on it and I am in contact with this community daily. I also have a Twitter account and reach out through that form of communication. I spend much time each day answering emails and reaching out to others through my email correspondence. I have also initiated a quarterly newsletter to stay in touch with my partners and those on my mailing list.[3] My television programs can be viewed anytime on demand at: www.frcedric.org/youtube. In order to be an effective minister of the Gospel, I feel you must be adept at relationships and communication, and social media plays a big role in that.

They Were of One Mind and Heart

The words "community" and "communication" are related. In order to build community there must be interaction and dialogue. The ten of us in my Passionist community live in close quarters. We pray together, eat together and spend leisure time together, and as a result, we get to know each other quite well. Sometimes one or another of us will take walks together or go out for a meal. These are bonding times that build intimacy and friendship.

When I work out at my fitness center, one of the exercises I enjoy is swimming, which gets every joint of the body involved and is good for the heart. The indoor fitness pool is a large one and it has five lanes. I've noticed

---

3 Email Jim@frcedric.org and we will send you the newsletter electronically.

that some people who are in the lanes on either side of me swim moderately and you hardly know they are there. Others make a big splash as they flail and kick, thus creating big waves. It is hard to swim and catch a breath when waves are coming at you. Every time we pass by each other, a spray of water and high waves hit me.

I think that life is like that situation in the pool. Most people you meet in life are reasonable, friendly and easy to get along with, and they don't create waves or make a splash. We have all had quiet, considerate neighbors who never bother anyone, but there are always people who splash water on you and create waves. They make life difficult. We all have experienced noisy, nosey neighbors with barking dogs who love to gossip. Most times, they aren't trying to create waves—it is just the way they are. We are the ones who have to deal with their spray of water and the waves they create. How you deal with others' wake is crucial to your own happiness. Try not to overreact, or you will live in misery.

Codependence

The term "codependence" is one term I became familiar with when I joined religious life. Codependence is when you base your own happiness or moods on the behavior of others. I found that I am very sensitive to the way people react to me, and I crave acceptance and am aware of how people respond to me. I want to be a witness to Jesus in my community living. When I preach, I want to inspire those I live with. When someone disagrees with me or is contentious it is very confusing to me. Perhaps a person leaves the room when I am talking or doesn't thank me for my homily after Mass. I keep thinking, "What did I do to make them like that?"

If you are a sensitive person you are more easily subject to codependence. I've produced television programs about relationships and codependence. While I am teaching I will have my producer show a puppet on strings being moved around by the puppeteer. That's how codependence works. You are codependent when you are controlled and manipulated by the moods and behaviors of others. You allow their disposition to determine your own happiness or well-being.

The area of codependence is crucial when dealing with addictive behaviors. When someone in your family or community is addicted to alcohol or another substance, everyone is affected. Relationships become dysfunctional and there is a lot of hurt and confusion. My training has taught me that when someone has the disease of alcoholism everyone in the family unit contracts the disease in some form. Those in the family unit may not drink, but they will catch the relationship dysfunction (lies, deceit, hurt, blame) that comes from the disease.

Al-Anon is an organization that is for spouses and family members of those who are addicted. These are people who have blamed themselves for their spouse's drinking and feel guilty, wondering if it was anything they did that caused their behavior. The self-blame and self-recrimination can be devastating. These family members aren't happy because they base their happiness on the way they are treated by the addicted family member. It is an endless cycle of trying to fix another person, and when they won't be fixed, it leads to a downward spiral on the part of the one trying to bring about the change.

I ran into this when I was stationed at one of our retreat centers as a seminarian. My ministry supervisor, who was a priest, was an alcoholic. He had been in recovery and wasn't drinking anymore, but he wasn't working his steps, either. This is called being a dry drunk. He was very controlling and we had a personality conflict. He became harsh and abusive toward me. At times he put me down verbally in front of others. I came from a family where my parents respected me and built me up. I knew I could always talk things out with them. I tried confronting him about his behavior and as I feared, he blew up in my face. He became defensive and even more explosive and angry. I was at a loss as to how to handle this relationship. The pain I experienced from this relationship led to learning about codependence.

I discovered I was basing my happiness and well-being on pleasing another person and being accepted by him. I found out that nothing I ever did was good enough. I couldn't "fix" him, so I learned I had to work on myself. I had to cut the strings, so to speak. The first line in the Serenity prayer by Reinhold Neibuhr is so crucial: "God grant me the serenity to accept the things I cannot change." I always want relationships neat and tidy. I want everyone to like me and be at peace, but relationships are not always under my control. They are complex and involve a lot of loose ends.

> *God grant me the serenity to accept the things I cannot change.*

As I have said, I have struggled with one of my two sisters since I was a young boy. For some reason she and I did not get along. It seemed no matter what I said or did, she took it the wrong way, and anything I tried to say to make it right made things even worse. We have had a strained relationship for years. I have tried to forgive and get along with her, but forgiveness isn't always reciprocal. After my mother died, she and I were forced to be together to work things out. While there were times of tension, there was also some compatibility. But there are also times where she didn't want to communicate. At times I feel like I am walking on thin ice around her. There are large gaps of silence in our communication. I can't control this. I can only leave the door open for further communication and not base my happiness on her moods. I must ask God to "grant me the serenity to accept the things (relationships) I cannot change." This is a repetitive prayer for me.

I hear similar things from parents who have a child who has moved away and won't communicate. Because the child doesn't want to relate, the parent lives in self-blame and deep melancholy. A woman who is a fervent believer came to me because her son became addicted, stole money from her and moved away. Needless to say, she was devastated. She tried to change him and she blamed herself over and over, to no avail. She is trying to cut the strings that bind her emotions to his dysfunctional behavior. Prayers are powerful, and God does hear the prayers of a mother. She keeps praying for her son. She is learning about her codependent emotions and how to find serenity in God. Being free from the unhappiness that comes from another's dysfunctional behavior is not easy. But neither is living under the guilt and self-recrimination of being unduly connected to someone who is addicted and doesn't care how you feel.

Life is all about relationships. The challenge of relationships is to reach greater heights. Forgive when you are harmed or misunderstood; don't be so touchy and easily offended; go the extra mile and communicate well; build intimacy even when you have to be the one to take the initiative. Don't allow the behaviors and manipulations and moods of others to control you. No one can make you feel one way or another—you choose to feel the way you do, and ultimately, you are responsible for your own feelings. We come out of our mother's womb connected and enmeshed by an umbilical cord. But in order for us to become an individual, the cord is cut right away. We are destined to be connected to others, but may sometimes have to cut the strings that manipulate us.

The Bible is a book about relationships. It focuses on our relationships with God, others and ourselves. We were created to be relational beings. The bottom line is, we cannot control all of the people in our lives. We must concentrate on ourselves and seek serenity. Relationships are a challenge, but these challenges can bring out the best in us and make us champions.

May God grant you happiness in your relationships. "May God, the source of all patience and encouragement, enable you to live in perfect harmony with one another…" (Ro. 15:6) As messy as relationships can be, they are a source of great joy. We were created to be related. I've always loved Psalm 133, which talks about how pleasant unity is:

Behold, how good and pleasant it is when people dwell in *unity!* It is like the precious oil upon the head, running down upon the beard, upon the beard of Aaron, running down on the collar of his robes! It is like the dew of Hermon, which falls on the mountains of Zion! For there the Lord has commanded the blessing, life for evermore.

EPILOGUE

In this book, I have demonstrated the truth that challenges make champions. Adversity can actually elevate us, weaknesses can make us winners, and problems can lead to promotion. These aren't just alliterative sayings. I have shown these phrases to be true over and over again. Whether it be physical problems, relationships, struggles with accomplishing dreams, or even your own death, in all these things we are more than conquerors through God who loves us.

There is an old Russian proverb that says, "The same hammer that shatters glass also forges steel." Your difficulties, misfortunes, troubles and sufferings can make you or break you. I have given abundant evidence that God works through trials to make us into the image of Jesus.

Unbroken

Some time ago, the local leader of our community in Houston recommended that I read a book called, *Unbroken*. Written by Laura Hillenbrand, the book was the story of Louis Zamperini. I was touched as I read about this war hero who faced suffering and challenges and came out on top.

Louis Zamperini was an American who became an Olympic track star. After the Olympics, he fought in World War II and his plane was shot down in the South Pacific. He almost died in the crash, but miraculously survived. He then had to face an unprecedented forty-seven days and nights in a raft. He was able to catch a bird with his own hands as well as a shark to eat, and through sheer willpower and determination, he fought to survive. Finally, he was found and captured by the Japanese and held as a prisoner of war for over two and a half year. At a camp in Tokyo, he was singled out by a violent head guard nicknamed the Bird, and tortured in humiliating and painful ways. Zamperini survived all of these horrors courageously and his spirit was unbroken.

After the war, he had flashbacks of the torture and experienced nightmares. He began drinking heavily, and his wife wanted a divorce. During the 1949 L.A. Billy Graham crusade he made good on a promise he made to God on the raft. He gave his life to Christ and his life turned around. His sufferings led him to God, who redeemed his life and gave him a new start. Louis's many challenges brought out the champion in him and would finally be the catalyst of a new relationship with God.

Louis Zamperini passed away at age ninety-seven in 2014. On Christmas, 2014, the movie *Unbroken*, directed by Angelina Jolie, was released. The movie was a great success and inspired many. I saw the movie and was greatly moved by it. It reaffirmed how strong our instinct to survive can be. There was one scene where Louis decided to kill the Bird after he was abused by the man countless times. He told one of his fellow prisoners of his plans to go out fighting and his comrade said, "If you attack him, he wins. *The way to victory is to endure and survive and outlast them.*" Louis changed his strategy and took his advice. He endured a multitude of tortures. Eventually, the U.S. won the war and Louis and his comrades were freed.

At the end of the movie, after all of his long trials and torments, Louis was finally reunited with his beloved parents. The reunion was one of the highlights of his new-found freedom. The embrace of his family was a glorious scene of triumph and victory that gave perspective to his sufferings.

Paul wrote, "We are knocked down, but not knocked out." Jesus taught, "By patient endurance you will win your soul."

The P.O.W. camp was an extreme example of what we all must endure now. We all have trials, sufferings and tribulations of every sort, and we must endure patiently for the time being; we can't give up or lose heart. One day we will triumph. Paul put it this way, "The sufferings of the present aren't worth comparing with the glory that will be revealed in (and to) us." (Ro. 8:18)

> *We all have trials, sufferings and tribulations of every sort.*

Angelina Jolie was interviewed about *Unbroken* and said, "Louie's story is all of our stories. He rose up in the midst of his sufferings and failings and so can we. What is this story all about? He faced every challenge and endured. When he was knocked down, he got back up. We've all had moments when we wanted to give up. Louie felt that too. But he fought back and refused to be taken down. Louie's story brings people together to push themselves to be their best."

Our story may not be as dramatic as surviving forty-seven days on a raft in the open Pacific, and we may not have had to endure the atrocities of a P.O.W. camp. Nor have we gone to the moon and back in a crippled spacecraft like the crew of Apollo 13. Most of us aren't blind and deaf like Helen Keller, we haven't lost legs to meningitis like Amy Purdy, or had to fight cancer like

Robin Roberts. But we all have challenges! If the people I have listed could allow their challenges to make them champions, we can allow our adversities to advance us as well. Our suffering can be a catalyst to form our character, develop our potential, and lead us to God. Don't waste your suffering—let it transform you. Life has much to teach us. We can't miss our own individualized life lessons. Our experiences are significant and they prepare us for our final challenge: our own death. In life and death God is with us to help us overcome in order *to* become.

> *Don't waste your suffering — let it transform you.*

Paul the Apostle has always been one of my heroes. As a missionary, he brought the Gospel to those who had never heard it. His call was fraught with various sufferings of every kind. As a present-day missionary who has to endure the travails of travel and preaching the Gospel, I am inspired by his life. In his writings he documents his imprisonments, beatings, shipwrecks, dangers, hunger, cold, exposure, and sleepless nights. Eventually, he would surrender his life to God through martyrdom in service of the Gospel. Through it all, he saw God's hand at work in his life, forming him, teaching him, and lifting him higher. Paul was passionate, resilient and pressed on, and because he fought the good fight, ran the race and finished his course unbroken, we are all beneficiaries of his indomitable spirit and compelling wisdom. His challenges made him a champion, and so must ours.

Toward the very end of his life Paul wrote these stirring words:

The time of my departure has come. I have fought the good fight, I have finished the race,

I have kept the faith. Henceforth there is laid up for me the crown of righteousness which the Lord, the just judge, will award to me on that Day, and not only to me but also to all who have loved his appearing. (2 Tim. 4:7-8)

I have given you many metaphors in this book. One of my favorites is that of the athlete running and finishing strong. I find it ironic that Louis Zamperini was an Olympic runner. The metaphor of training and racing for the prize served him well.

One of our Passionist priests was a marathon runner. During one of his races he got so tired and felt so bad physically he gave up and quit running in the middle of the race. He told me, "I never forgave myself for stopping."

We must endure and not give up! The Bible tells us, "Do you not know that in a race all the runners compete but only one receives the prize? *Run that you may win.* Athletes compete to receive a perishable crown, but we a crown that is *imperishable.*" (1 Cor. 9:24-25)

Although the race is hard and we must endure sufferings of every sort, the finish line will be so worth it! Keep running the race and know that your sufferings have great value and are making you worthy. Endurance and the ability to persevere is of utmost importance in the Bible. The writer of Hebrews imagines a scene in a large stadium at the end of a marathon. He encourages us by telling us we are "surrounded by a great cloud of witnesses...let us run the race with perseverance." (Heb. 12:1) The angels, saints and those who have gone before us are watching and praying for us. The contest we are in now determines eternity. Run to win! Your challenges and hardships will make you a champion.

ABOUT THE AUTHOR

Fr. Cedric Pisegna, C.P. is a Passionist priest who professed vows in September 1985. He was born in Springfield, Massachusetts and graduated from the University of Massachusetts at Amherst with B.S. in social work and a minor in Business. In addition, he has studied Philosophy at Southern Illinois University and has studied Speech and Drama at Northwestern University in Chicago. Fr. Cedric graduated from the Catholic Theological Union at Chicago in May 1990, receiving his Master of Divinity degree with Bible Specialization. He was ordained a priest on June 29, 1991.

Presently, Fr. Cedric preaches retreats and missions throughout the United States and Canada, ministering out of the Passionist retreat complex in Houston, Texas. He has preached over 400 missions for 25 years. Fr. Cedric produces a program for TV and Radio, *Live with Passion!*, which presently airs nationally and internationally on the Trinity Broadcasting Network (TBN) and other networks. He has numerous CDs and DVDs on Christian living and has authored twenty books.

If you wish to contact Father Cedric write or email:

Email: frcedric@frcedric.org
Website: www.frcedric.org

It is my intent to give credit for use of copyrighted material contained in this book. If such credit has inadvertently been omitted, please contact me at frcedric@frcedric.org so subsequent printings will contain the appropriate acknowledgment.

INSPIRATIONAL RESOURCES BY FR. CEDRIC PISEGNA, C.P.

Books:
1 Live Passionately!
2 Glorious Holy Spirit
3 Thy Kingdom Come!
4 You Can Change
5 Death: The Final Surrender
6 Come Encounter Jesus
7 Golf & God
8 Eucharist: A Living Sacrifice
9 God's Not Boring!
10 A Retreat with Fr. Cedric
11 He Touched Me
12 You Can Be Happy: A Lifestyle of Well-Being
13 Kept in Christ
14 Seasons of Life
15 The Sacred Walk
16 Choose Life and Live!
17 Rise! Living the Risen Life
18 You Are Loved!
19 Challenges Make Champions
20 More Than A Conqueror

Additional Inspirational Teaching Series:
Fr. Cedric has produced hundreds of CDs and DVDs that will deepen your relationship with God and inspire you to Live with Passion!

To place an order online or for a complete listing of Fr. Cedric's teachings visit www.frcedric.org/bookstore

For ordering by mail contact:
Fr Cedric Ministries ● 430 Bunker Hill Rd
Houston TX 77024 ● 844-328-4372
Email:Jim@frcedric.org ● Website:www.frcedric.org

THE CONGREGATION OF THE PASSION

The Passionists are a religious community in the Catholic Church. They were founded in 1741 in Italy. The founder of the Passionists was Paul Daneo (St. Paul of the Cross). Their headquarters is in Rome, Italy. They are in 60 countries around the world. The major ministry of the Passionist priests, brothers and sisters is prayer and evangelization.

A Passionist religious professes vows of poverty, chastity, and obedience. Along with these is the unique first vow of a Passionist: to remember and meditate upon the Passion of Jesus and to proclaim its meaning to the world. The sign that Passionists wear on their religious habit (Jesu XPI Passio) means "The Passion of Jesus Christ." A familiar saying of Passionists is: "May the Passion of our Lord be always in our hearts."

For more information about the Passionists or if you are interested in a religious vocation, please contact:

Vocation Director
Passionist Community
773-631-6336

Websites:
www.passionist.org
www.frcedric.org